WOMANCHRIST

L Nadeau

WomanChrist

A New Vision of Feminist Spirituality

Christin Lore Weber

PERENNIAL LIBRARY

Harper & Row, Publishers, San Francisco

Cambridge, Hagerstown, New York, Philadelphia, Washington
London, Mexico City, São Paulo, Singapore, Sydney

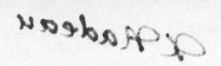

Grateful acknowledgment is given for use of the following: From "if i have, mylady, intricate" in *IS 5 poems*, by e.e. cummings. Copyright © 1985 by e.e. cummings Trust. Copyright © 1926 by Horace Liveright. Copyright © 1954 by e.e. cummings. Copyright © 1985 by George James Firmage. Reprinted by permission of Liveright Publishing Corporation. From "The Dry Salvages" in *Four Quartets*, by T. S. Eliot. Copyright 1943 by T. S. Eliot; renewed 1971 by Esme Valerie Eliot. Reprinted by permission of Harcourt Brace Jovanovich, Inc. From "The Waste Land" in *Collected Poems 1909–1962*, by T. S. Eliot. Copyright 1936 by Harcourt Brace Jovanovich, Inc.; copyright © 1963, 1964 by T. S. Eliot. Reprinted by permission of the publisher. From *A Hopkins Reader*, by Gerard Manley Hopkins, edited by John Pick. Copyright 1966. Reprinted by permission of Image Books, Doubleday and Co. From *Dark Soliloquy: The Selected Poems of Gertrud Kolmar*, by Gertrud Kolmar. Translated and with an Introduction by Henry A. Smith. English translation © 1975 by The Continuum Publishing Company. Reprinted by permission of The Continuum Publishing Company. "Prepatriarchal Female/Goddess Images" from *The Politics of Woman's Spirituality*, by Adrienne Rich, editied by Charlene Spretnak. Copyright © 1982. Reprinted by permission of Anchor Books, Anchor Press/Doubleday. From "The God-Monger" in *The Awful Rowing Toward God*, by Anne Sexton. Copyright © 1975 by Loring Conant, Jr., Executor of Estate of Anne Sexton. Reprinted by permission of Houghton Mifflin Company. From *Surfacing*, by Margaret Atwood. Copyright © 1972 by Margaret Atwood. Reprinted by permission of Simon & Schuster, Inc. From *The White Goddess*, by Robert Graves. Copyright © 1948 by International Authors, N.V. Reprinted by permission of Farrar, Straus and Giroux, Inc. From *Inanna: Queen of Heaven and Earth*, by Diane Wolkstein and Samuel Noah Kramer. Copyright © 1983 by Diane Wolkstein and Samuel Noah Kramer. Reprinted by permission of Harper & Row, Publishers, Inc. From *Meditations with Hildegard of Bingen*, by Gabrile Uhlein. Copyright © 1982 by Bear & Company. Reprinted by permission. From *Meditations with Mechtild of Magdeburg*, by Sue Woodruff. Copyright © 1982 by Bear & Company. Reprinted by permission.

WOMANCHRIST. Copyright © 1987 by Christin Lore Weber. All rights reserved. Printed in the United States of America. No part of this book may be used or reproduced in any manner whatsoever without written permission except in the case of brief quotations embodied in critical articles and reviews. For information address Harper & Row, Publishers, Inc., 10 East 53rd Street, New York, NY 10022. Published simultaneously in Canada by Fitzhenry & Whiteside, Limited, Toronto.

FIRST EDITION

Library of Congress Cataloging-in-Publication Data

Weber, Christin Lore.
  Womanchrist : a new vision of feminist spirituality.

  1. Women—Religious life.   2. Spirituality.
3. Weber, Christin Lore.   I. Title.
BV4527.W39   1987   248.8'43   87-45199
ISBN 0-06-254830-1

90 91 RRD 10 9 8 7 6 5 4 3

To the generations of women in my family:

Krista May, daughter of
Elizabeth Anne, daughter of
Alyce Rose, daughter of
Elizabeth Catherine, daughter of
Maria.

Contents

Preface

Christianity forms an essential part of my history and my culture, and its images and mysteries are rooted deep in my soul. From the beginning of my consciousness I have attempted to wed those Christian archetypes with other natural energies constellated in my psychic depths. I have desired to be both woman and Christian. As the years progress and I discover more about who I am as woman, I find I need to be more and more discriminating about the accumulated traditions, rituals, and moral codes of the Christian Church in all of its various denominational manifestations. At the same time, my love for the person Jesus was, my belief in his continuing life, my fascination with the manner in which he broke open the human to reveal our power of life, my love for and sense of connectedness with the women who have seen through to the truth of his message—Julian of Norwich, Hildegard of Bingen, Mechtild of Magdeburg, and Mary of Magdala, from the past, and Alla, Bethany, Ruth, and Sister Marie Nativity, from my present—all draw me deeper into the mystery of Christianity's origins in him. I take my place as a woman in the movement of creation that Jesus revealed and attempt from the perspective of my experience and the experiences of the women who surround me to re-vision and reconstruct a Christian spirituality of women's mysteries.

The exploration to the Beginning has taken me from an idyllic and contemplative childhood on the shores of Lake of the Woods in Minnesota to a convent on the prairies of America's heartland, to Wisdom House in St. Paul, and finally to a restful valley on the California coast. I have been drawn by Love into the mystery of nature, the traditions of the Church, the complexities of religious community life, the intricacies of a theological education, the intimacy of marriage, the sacred metamorphosis of widowhood, and the souls of the children and adults I have encountered as spiritual director and pastoral counselor.

This book is sometimes a journal, sometimes a story, sometimes a study, sometimes a poem. It records my own spiritual searching for connections and my reflections on the searching of women I have known and with whom I have shared life. The re-visioning is happening in all of our lives every day. I hope this book can invite and encourage women and men to look deeply and see the connections—Christ in woman and woman in Christ.

Acknowledgments

A book such as this one can be written only with the aid and support of many people. Only because women were willing to share their lives and stories with me was it possible for me to formulate the image of WomanChrist. Consequently, I wish to acknowledge, first of all, the women of the Wisdom House Community. As clients, members of our worship group, supporters of our endeavor, and friends, these women offered me the spiritual, emotional, and psychological gifts that are woven into an intricate pattern of womanbody/womansoul and womanpower/womanwisdom throughout this book.

I also wish to acknowledge those women whose lives contributed to my personal understanding of what it means to be both woman and Christian. These are women who have known me intimately: in my family, especially my mother, Alyce Lore, and my sister, Elizabeth Kensinger; and my teachers, particularly Sister Marie Schwan, Sister Ella Jean Carufel, Sister Marie Nativity, Sister Marie Leon, and Evelyn Jesme.

In the production and publication of *WomanChrist* I am indebted to my editor, Jan Johnson, for her astute critique, understanding, and encouragement. I am grateful to friends and colleagues who listened, questioned, and urged me on during the writing process: Suzanne Swanson, Kathleen Jesme, Beverly Kelly, and Alla Bozarth. Finally, I shall always be grateful to Jim Campbell who appeared miraculously in my life and introduced the *WomanChrist* manuscript to Harper & Row.

Most important of all is John, my spouse. He believed in me. He held me when I wept with discouragement. He celebrated each success. He carried me through.

Part One

WOMANBODY, WOMANSOUL

In describing individuals in counseling sessions or situations I have changed all names, characteristics, and identifying details.

CHAPTER 1

Opening the Passage

Spring struggles to be born this year. Yesterday's May winds rattled our storm windows, bent the young branches of our birch tree almost to the ground, and whipped round me with a threat of snow. Even the squirrels hid, and birds sought shelter under the eves. At night I dreamed a law was passed requiring me to return to the convent; the sisters locked me in a room of earth and stone at the bottom of a dark tunnel and, smiling, said I would adjust. I wept. I awoke from sleep, weeping.

This morning brought sunshine but no relief from chilling wind. As I sat warming my hands on the smooth, comfortable surface of my coffee mug, I began to notice that despite the persistent cold the large elms had opened in canopies of thin golden green. Spring flowed up through passages in earth and tree to burst in delicacy against the blue sky. Faintly, as from a distance, I heard, then, the song of birds, their calling opening some passageway in me, and I remembered Judith.

Judith died at dawn. "Listen, Judith," I had said but a moment before, "the birds are singing; it is another day." She was forty-eight. I reached over to the vase beside her bed in the hospice, removed a daisy, and placed it on the pillow beside her head. Later, in the privacy of my home, I grieved not only for her death but also for her desperate struggle to give life to her sons, and for their refusal to receive. I grieved for her desolation. I grieved for the absence of her sons at her deathbed. I grieved for her years of stoic courage to stay alive for them. I grieved for her resistance to death and her anticipation of their presence to the very end. I grieved for the years of her uncomplaining silence, the secrets she kept, the betrayals she endured. I grieved for myself, my own death, all the closed passageways in me that could be opened only through an inexorable rending of my soul.

She is sister to my soul. We have been bonded by companionship on the passage through death. I came with her to the very boundary, holding her hand, singing songs against the dark, until she pulled her hand away and continued alone beyond breath.

In our encounters during the years since we had met—first in spiritual guidance sessions to prepare her for the death that was expected within a year, and then in cafés month after month for four years, because she defied death—I learned, really, very little about Judith. She married young, against the wishes of her parents; bore three sons; suffered the desertion of her spouse; divorced; married again; felt rejected by her church; discovered that her second spouse was a drug runner; divorced again; guarded her sons against their stepfather lest they be formed according to his image, with his skills; was found to have cancer; suffered two radical mastectomies; was uprooted from her home in the East to live with relatives "so she could be cared for"; experienced the slow, sure spread of the cancer to bone, to eyes, to lungs, to brain; decided to live until her youngest son was eighteen years old; worried about what would happen to her cat when she was dead.

She had learned well the lesson of secrecy: how not to open the passages to feelings, how to guard the way into the depths. The secrecy of pain, of abandonment, of not feeling loved. Her longing, her devotion, her need for faith in God and in herself remained untold. With laughter, matter-of-fact voice, studied posture, careful makeup she constructed a facade against a world of hurt. And she kept her secrets until the sixteen hours I was with her before her death, when her body was broken and she no longer had a voice. Then, somehow, the secrets found a passageway into her eyes and I could see them all. She knew it and she let me see.

THE PASSAGE

Before all else, women's spirituality depends on an open passage within, a free channel for the flow of life and the creative birthing of a continually renewed self. We learn about passage before we can think. The absolute requirement of an open passage seems to imprint itself in our every cell even before our own births, and the journey we make down through the birth canal of our mothers creates an impression of ease or difficulty in passage that, I think, our souls never forget. The unconscious memory of the birth passage rises in dream imagery as well as in our willingness for or resistance to the lifelong urging of our souls to pass into wider being.

We encounter the mystery of passage again through the experience of menstruation. Our bodies open to the flow of life-blood. The control we achieved over bodily functions as children is useless against the blood flow; we release. We may try to hold ourselves against the flow of blood; we cramp down and feel the pain of our bodies holding back, but we cannot prevent this passage of life.

There are extreme occasions, when the soul perceives mortal danger, that the blood flow is stopped, also in a manner beyond our conscious control. Women in the German death camps experienced the cessation of their menstrual cycles. Sometimes one woman perceives mortal danger in the day-to-day passage of her life. Women who have survived incest or childhood violence, for example, feel so strong a need to keep the pain of that experience from surfacing into their consciousness that their attempt to keep down the flow of memory can affect the body's flow of blood. A client of mine thought she might be pregnant since her menstrual periods had stopped, but the tests were negative. When she was able to release the secret of her childhood pain, the flow of blood was released with it.

The opening of the passage that we begin to learn with the onset of menstruation joins us to the natural process of passage in all of nature. The passage is cyclical. We begin to experience our connection with the cycles of the moon, of day and night, of the seasons in the earth, of the ebb and flow of tides. In our souls, our psychic bodies, we feel the movement of cosmic life so that our spirits feel in connection with the energy of all creation. Women's spirituality is nature-based, earth-grounded, cosmic consciousness. Our God is cosmic. Natural. We experience union with God in creation's process of cycling life in ourselves and in all that surrounds us. The entire cosmos is a passage of the ineffable Mystery of Being we call God containing and contained by us. Our spirituality needs the opening of the passage in order to flow, and we are taught this by our blood and by our breath.

After we descended the birth passage of our mothers and emerged in the wider world, a cry opened the passage for our breath. Our breathing empowers us not only to live but to be aware of the depth and Mystery of life, teaching us in every moment the cycle of filling and emptying essential to spirituality.

Spirituality is awareness of our oneness with the breath of the universe, of the creative rhythm of God. In the taking in and the letting go of breath we are the flow and ebb of creation, which alternates blessing with pain. The more we take in the love and blessing of the Holy Creative Mystery, the more sensitive we become to the labor of creation, the pain of the cosmos, the cry of birth that frees the breath of the earth and her people.

The deeper we breathe in, the more aware we are of the emptying. The breathing in becomes a spirituality of delighting, of being filled with blessing, of passion for a more full coming to be, of our individual selves and of all creation. So the breathing in becomes a com-passion, a participation in the openness of all creation to receive the fullness of God.

And the breathing out becomes an emptying of all that is not God, a letting go of all that weighs us down and separates us from the wholeness of the cosmos. In breathing out we are connected to the emptiness in our world so that through us can flow the blessing of God, which, again, is compassion.

Our spirituality actually originates in our bodily breath of life. As we develop we become aware of our participation in the creative breathing of the Holy Cosmic Mystery bringing all that is to birth. This cosmic creative Breath is the Holy Spirit.

Our bodies and the earth itself teach that such participation in the Breath of the Holy Cosmic Mystery means a paradox of ebb and flow, of fullness of delight and of emptying, of intense compassion and letting go to simplicity, of blessing and of pain. Our spirituality can never be isolated and individualistic, since the essence of its energy connects us to and grounds us in creation, in which, and as a part of which, we come to know and live out the Spirit of God. Our opening not only creates a passageway for God; it makes us who we really are—the freely moving creative energy of cosmic Mystery. We are the passage. We are the Being.

BLOCKING THE PASSAGE

Judith kept the secret of herself lest she be discovered to be unworthy of love, her vulnerable soul invaded and then abandoned. I don't know what causes cancer in the body; I do know that Judith's secrets calcified in her soul and blocked the passageways of her life. She washed her rejection daily in the salt water of pain and then fastened it firmly into the passageway of her soul, where it stopped up the flow of spirit to her being. She thought of it as courage.

She did let go at last, but only in death; and the beauty of her flooded up into her eyes. In holding down the secret of her pain, she also had held down the secret of her beautiful self. It is significant to me that she chose a passage from Colleen McCullough's novel *The Thorn Birds* to be read at her funeral.

There is a legend about a bird which sings just once in its life, more sweetly than any other creature on the face of the earth. From the moment it leaves the nest it searches for a thorn tree, and does not rest until it has found one. Then singing among the savage branches, it impales itself upon the longest, sharpest spine. And, dying, it rises above its own agony to out-carol the lark and the nightingale. One superlative song, existence the price. But the whole world stills to listen and God in His heaven smiles. For the best is only brought at great pain. . . . Or so says the legend.[1]

Judith knew about the ebb and flow. She knew about opening the passage by letting go of imposed secrets so that the secret of life and its mystery could flow forth and be revealed. But why did she need to learn it at so extravagant a price? Why could only death release the mysterious song?

There is a paradox here, for it is the secret we keep in order to survive that becomes a cancer blocking the flow of life and threatening our destruction. And at the core of every secret we keep is one that since the times of matrifocal cultures and religions it has been taboo to speak. It is the secret of our power.

These are two of the ways we have held the secret of our

power against ourselves: by silencing our voice and by denying our vision.

SILENCING OUR VOICE

During the summer of 1964, just after graduating from college, I taught speech and drama to a group of novices at a convent in the Midwest. The biggest challenge I experienced was helping them find their voices. Although these women were adults in their early twenties, their voices maintained the high, breathy quality of the small girl-child. No power there. These women had disembodied their voices and unempowered the expression of their thoughts. By so doing, they seemed to assume a submissive attitude every time they spoke, and the more they spoke the more submissive they seemed to become.

All summer we exercised those voices, using tape recorders, body exercises, breathing exercises, yelling exercises—finding the body's center, finding the voice's source. At the summer's end, not only did the voices sound different—grounded, strong, assured—but the women themselves were different. They had begun to locate a passageway to their power.

DENYING OUR VISION

Some years ago when my spouse and I took a trip to Ireland, we included in our itinerary a visit to a woods in which ancient Druids are thought to have lived and worshiped. We separated as we explored the narrow pathways, and I found myself alone where sunlight filtered through the thick green leaves of giant yew trees. Between the carved-out walls of living rock, stairs descended into a kind of sacred cave into which light flowed through a round hole open to the sky. As I made my way into this earth womb I felt the presence of the ancient women who had walked this way before me; I felt their power; I knew my oneness with them. It was a surprise encounter with the ever-present past, something that I could not have planned but that worked a transformation in my soul, bonding me with these women beyond the confines of time.

Coming out of the cave and into the cool green filtered light, I was aware of a cleansing fear and a magnificent fullness of power. From a bush I picked a small triangular leaf and placed it carefully in my New Testament, not knowing why but sensing a significance in my action. It remains there today as a promise of connections between the Druidic profession of faith as hymned in Robert Graves's reconstruction of an ancient group of poems: the "Câd Goddeu: A Battle of Trees" and something I have known as a woman about a Christian feminist spirituality.

> I have been in many shapes,
> Before I attained a congenial form.
> I have been a narrow blade of a sword.
> (I will believe it when it appears.)
> I have been a drop in the air.
> I have been a shining star.
> I have been a word in a book.
> I have been a book originally.
> I have been a light in a lantern.
> A year and a half.
> I have been a bridge for passing over
> Three-score rivers.
> I have journeyed as an eagle.
> I have been a boat on the sea.
> I have been a director in battle.
> I have been the string of a child's swaddling clout.
> I have been a sword in the hand.
> I have been a shield in the fight.
> I have been the string of a harp,
> Enchanted for a year
> In the foam of water.
> I have been a tree in a covert.
> There is nothing in which I have not been.[2]

Through the Irish Druid garden I *see*. I do not know exactly *what* I see nor do I know the meaning of the vision entirely. I suspect it has something to do with T. S. Eliot's hints and guesses in "The Dry Salvages":

> For most of us, there is only the unattended
> Moment, the moment in and out of time,
> The distraction fit, lost in a shaft of sunlight,
> The wild thyme unseen, of the winter lightning
> Or the waterfall, or music heard so deeply
> That it is not heard at all, but you are the music
> While the music lasts. These are only hints and guesses,
> Hints followed by guesses; and the rest

Is prayer, observance, discipline, thought and action.
The hint half guessed, the gift half understood is Incarnation.[3]

Incarnation. There is nothing in which we have not been. Everything is connected in the ebbing and flow of life. We are the music.

TELLING OUR SECRETS AND RELEASING OUR POWER

If I return to the time in my own life before the oppression of secrecy, I am at Lake of the Woods in Minnesota. Some women remember no time before oppression. They are women who have always kept secrets against themselves, who are aware of no vision of their own, no creative truth that they can tell. But most of us have something: northern lights in an inky sky, a tree-house shelter, an uncle who took you walking by the ocean, a teacher who chose you to help her in the classroom, a grandmother who invited you to a tea party in her parlor once a week and who sent you off filled with cookies and love.

My grandmother is the Lake. As a small child I sat on a hillock at her edge and learned from her the secrets of life. She breathed with the wind, laughed sunlight, and crashed upon the rock-piled shore during each dark, vast summer storm. After her anger, though, she left on the sand deposits of arrowheads from times before my life began, and diamond willow that drifted in from her fourteen thousand islands.

The waves of her breath provided rhythm for my own breathing, which made its way into my soul's center unawares. Her waters surround the most ancient rock outcroppings on the earth: granite from prehistoric times, on which pine trees now shade blueberries for the deer and bear. Her sands as well as her rocks are white and black, her sandy beaches' powder fine and warm.

Winters, she creates wonders of ice craggy against the shore. We would drive the truck out on her cold, solid surface to cut ice for storing until summer in the sawdust of the icehouse on the edge of the woods. Ice—gigantic cubes of brilliant amber.

She contains mystery, both comforting and dangerous. People have died in her because they lacked respect, assuming control where one cannot be in control but must learn her language and respond humbly to her power. She cannot be fought; if we respect her, we develop compassion within her power.

One night when I was four years old, a boat did not return to a resort down the road. Storm clouds darkened the moon, and searchlights picked up whitecaps foaming atop eight-foot waves. My Grandmother Klimek alerted each cabin and resort from Wheeler's Point to Morris Point by ringing each code on the old phone—two shorts and a long, two longs and three shorts, a short and a long. All the frantic adults had forgotten me as I sat terrified and fascinated on the black leather sofa in the lounge of Klimek's Lodge listening to the wind's roar and the waves' crash, mingled with the cacophony of adults calling orders, whispering in corners, weeping with fear for those lost. I don't remember if the boat was found. I don't remember when someone noticed me and put me to bed. I do remember the power of my Lake and my awesome respect for her.

Her beauty was unsurpassed. From the beach at Morris Point she stretched to vastness, to the end of the world. Off to the right, Pine Island sheltered coves for the fisherfolk to find the walleyed and northern pike. Returning to her once with my friend and mentor, Sister Marie, I witnessed the rising of charcoal-colored storm clouds over the island and the sun creating three rainbows above her, connecting island to mainland in the distance. One gull flew through the arch.

When I was seventeen years old and leaving for convent life, I went to her on my last night home. An enormous wind had riled her so that her voice drowned out all other sounds. I found my way alone from the car to the beach and stood engulfed by wave sounds, whipped by wind, crying, my tears mixing with hers sprayed on my face.

She is my grandmother. She is in my bodysoul. She is what I know of life—its birthing, terror, beauty, and surprise, its depth and width. She is the source of wisdom, nourishment, and compassion. She is where I will return in death.

From her I received my voice.

Only when we find the voices we need to speak our vision will we release our power and cease holding secrets against ourselves. To give voice to our visions we will need to let go of some culturally imposed expectations that seem designed to limit our truth and minimize our experience. Primary among these expectations is that of "making sense." By "making sense" our patriarchal culture means fitting into its externally imposed system of logic, its rationale for the life process, its worldview that often does not encompass our experience.

I have a friend who telephones me at least once a week with an experience of life that "doesn't fit." Each time we talk she begins with embarrassed explanations designed to prepare me for listening to something she feels she must keep secret from everyone else lest they find her "crazy." She almost always includes the admonition "Please don't mind if I don't make sense, now, but . . ."

The stories she tells always contain an element of mystery, an interpretation of life that is based on direct personal experience and that combines the following elements: synchronicity, the chance co-incidence of disparate happenings that mysteriously fit together in a manner that gives meaning to some question in her life; earthy intuition, a rising sense of belief grounded in a direct sensual experience of reality; self-containment, a strong and peaceful acceptance of the many-faceted self; and numinosity, the entire experience taking place within the context of cosmic, beneficent, and holy Mystery, which is ultimately inexplicable.

My friend, you, me, all of us, if we are to discover our spirituality, must trust our experience even when it doesn't seem to "make sense." The logic needs to flow out of the experience rather than be imposed on it as a judgment. We must voice our visions and tell our stories to one another withholding judgment, allowing the meaning to be revealed organically as the vision increases and the story winds on. The process will be frightening sometimes because it will contradict prevailing worldviews, but if we continue to keep our secrets against ourselves, not only ourselves will be destroyed. The experiences of our lives are gifts with which to create the future of the world; the power we release by giving voice to those gifts is meant to transform us all. We need to be willing to not "make sense" within a world where our experience does not fit, and by so doing to bring to being a world that fits our experience.

We may wonder what the power is that we have kept secret for so long. Many have speculated about this—a power that is communal, circular, mutual, cooperative, rather than elitist, hierarchical, dominating, and competitive.

I expect our power is all this and more, but it remains largely hidden in the secrets of the world's women. It will be released as the secrets are told, are accepted, are celebrated and made creative of a new vision, a new spiritual energy.

Each of us has an icon that forms the passageway for our power, and part of our spiritual search is to recognize it. The icon of my friend Alla is a mountain she calls her Medicine Woman. It is through the mountain that her power is conducted and her secrets told and deepened. Judith's icon became the thorn bird, to release the power secreted away for a lifetime in a triumphant song at death. Had her icon been a different one that had compelled her earlier to cease keeping secrets against herself, might she be alive today? No one knows.

My Grandmother Lake is an icon telling me who I was, am, and will become. She is my soul. I feel my boundaries expand to her limits, and I know her moods and the wisdom of her ancient being. She tells my secret and in the telling releases power while deepening the secret for a further telling.

CHAPTER 2

Remembering the Mysteries

What women know has been formed through complex interconnections of our history and our biology, neither of which is causative of what we are nor determines what we shall become, but both of which provide us with a perspective from which to interpret our own reality and the meaning of universal reality. Biologically, we have been the birth givers. Historically, we have, on the one hand, founded civilizations and religions, and, on the other, been oppressed, marginalized, misinterpreted, and ignored by patriarchal power-based systems. Each of us carries the memory of our combined past, and the memory is long and deep.

We remember that we orginated life, bore new being within ourselves, fascinated people by our awesome power in those times before the male role in the life process was imagined. We remember connecting our cycles of blood with the cycles of the moon, which led to the telling of time and the passage of the seasons. We have been shamans of life's mysteries and originators of world cultures. We who knit together the bones and flesh of human beings within our wombs also wove the baskets for storing and carrying food—seeds to begin agriculture, herbs for healing. We who severed the umbilical cords to free new persons into life also sat in the tribal circle formed to make the decisions that bound and severed relationships according to community justice. We worshiped the power of life itself, imaging her as the birthing, nourishing, sustaining Goddess whose weaving created the universe and whose just severing brought death in its time to serve the cycle of being.

Eventually the gods changed and women's mysteries became

buried in the darkness of every person's unconscious psyche—in the collective unconscious of human being. With the power of life itself buried, other kinds of power could thrive: power to take control, power to conquer, power to rule over, power to make slaves, power to make war. Replacing the circle of justice was the throne of the king who wielded judgment with an elaborate system of rules formulated to substitute for humankind's connectedness to the fundamental process of life.

We remember the oppression: exclusion from decision making that affected the whole community, minimization of our roles in the development of thought and culture, exclusion of our viewpoint from recorded history. We remember rape, brutalization, domination. We remember learning the survival techniques of secrecy, seduction, and manipulation. We remember wishing we were men, taking on the power of patriarchy, repressing our own mysteries, contributing to world domination in a mistaken notion that such was the way to the power of life. We were wrong. Where we still believe this, we remain wrong.

When we remember women's mysteries, what women know, we need to take into consideration all dimensions of our history and biology, sort out and differentiate the creative from the destructive forces, allow ourselves to learn from both, and then articulate the knowledge. This process is central to women's spirituality and to a more holistic spirituality of the human. The memory of the feminine is rising in human consciousness—that of both women and men—and this emergence will transform everything. Carl Jung thought that Pope Pius XII's declaration of the Assumption of Mary foretold a world consciousness of the archetypal feminine rising from the bowels of the earth where she had been buried during centuries of androcentric power and authority. She images the Goddess, rising with the power of life, to transform the God of the clouds and bring unity and wholeness to being. In Mary's Assumption, Jung perceived Sophia (divine, feminine Wisdom) reunited with the Godhead.

Each theme of women's spirituality enables us to reach into the depths of our experience for the hidden, corresponding mystery, to raise it up and assume it into our consciousness, and then, out of that more complete consciousness, to allow our perspective to be transformed. It is from such a transformed perspective that re-visioning of a Christian spirituality in the light of women's mysteries can take place. The first theme, that of passage, engages us in the women's mystery of ebb and flow.

THE MYSTERY OF EBB AND FLOW

We have learned of life that it is not only linear but also cyclical. Creation does not continually increase to produce more and better; rather, it is a mystery of ebb and flow. Androcentric consciousness does not want to remember this mystery and has taught us to distrust our experience, to accept instead a kind of drivenness toward increase. The popular affirmation, "Every day, in every way, I am getting better and better," stands as a strong reminder of what we "should" think and how we "should" be.

Occasionally, ebb and flow are recognized as inescapably part of the life process, but the ebb is treated as something to be endured while we await the next flow. If we could experience life as a process of circling, winding, spiraling in and out of itself in a creative dance of being, we would know that ebbing and flowing counterbalance one another in the dance, both necessary to the spiraling rhythm. The passage of life is an intricate one that, if it is to be kept open, requires the continual ebbing of one energy so that another may flow, balanced by the ebbing of the second to give flow to the first.

The womanbody event of our menstrual cycle can give us a womansoul perspective on the ebb-flow mystery if we are willing to trust our experience. Like most women, I was educated to believe that the psychophysiological rhythm of this cycle was a handicap to be overcome. As an adolescent I noticed with fascination the surge and decline of creative energy as I lived through a monthly cycle. At the time of menstrual flow, my emotional energy ebbed and I experienced a profound sense of quiet withdrawal during which it seemed I contemplated a mystery I shared with the Lake, the rain, the earth. However, I remember being chided for my withdrawal, teased into social response, goaded into angry reactions, and then minimized with "Well, it's no wonder you're so touchy—it's your time of the month!" or "What is wrong with you? Is it *your time?*" As the spiral dance of my body proceeded toward the period of ovulation, emotional energy flowed, creative ideas emerged, social engagement flourished. My contemplative side ebbed and I lost an intimate sense of myself in connection with the allness of life. At these times I would hear, "You seem so happy these days; why can't you be like this all the time?" I learned that I was acceptable only during those times of creative and emotional flow—times when I was not menstruating. My psychological state during menstruation needed to be overcome, overpowered by a pretended gaiety, a courageous social involvement, a careful guarding of my rapidly evolving sense of inadequacy to accomplish the task of living.

It was my spouse who led me back to my self. Early in our relationship he shared with me a marvelous wonder over the cyclical experience of women and expressed his feeling that if he could experience his own body in such a manner, he would have a personal understanding of the cosmic processes: "Your body is a microcosm of the universe, your menstrual period like the tides of great oceans drawn by the moon."

We ebb and flow, life ebbs and flows, the entire cosmos is a process of ebb and flow, and the ebbing is as holy as the flow. This is the mystery we need to remember and believe. This ancient mystery can be found codified in philosophies of world religions and expressed through works of wisdom such as the Chinese Book of Changes, the *I Ching,* which is based on the principles of yin and yang—cosmic moving patterns of decrease and increase, ebb and flow. Never can the one be found without the other, and the one is always in the process of becoming the other.

Perhaps we will rediscover the secret of our power when we can finally raise up from our depths the wisdom of ebb and flow. Ebbing has been called weakness, but perhaps we will discover in it a new kind of power. Perhaps there is power in all that we have associated with the ebb side of the cycle: silence, waiting, emptiness, darkness, receptivity, detachment, aloneness, and death. Perhaps ebbing is the power opening the passage through which life flows. Perhaps, paradoxically, emptying *is* fullness.

I wonder again about Judith. Did it take the ebbing we call death in all its power to finally open for her a passage large enough for the flow of her life? All other ebbing she rejected and fought because it resulted from the pain, the abuse, and the abandonment. She controlled the energy slipping away, said it wasn't happening. Death she could not control. She finally let go to the ebbing away of everything and, mysteriously, by that process released a flow beyond imagination. We who were with her could see life rising in her face as she engaged in her dying. We could hear her exultant creative song through the voices of the awakening birds. There was power in that room, then, beyond any I had ever before known. This woman who was dying was dangerous with power, and we were all silent before her mystery.

A RE-VISIONING OF THE DEATH-RESURRECTION MYSTERY

The central mystery of Christian faith is that Jesus, though he died, lives. Significantly, it is in the recording of this mystery in the Scriptures that women figure most strongly. One Good Friday when I was a child, I was too ill to attend the afternoon liturgy. Instead, my mother cuddled me on her lap in the old wicker rocking chair and softly told me the story of how Jesus died. Scripture entwined with folktale in her rendition, and we were there with him and his faithful women friends: the wife of Pilate, who dreamed about the innocence of the condemned man and pleaded with her husband to spare him; the women of Jerusalem, who crowded near to him as he carried his cross and who wept for his pain and their loss; the brave Veronica, who stepped from the jeering crowd to comfort him by wiping the blood and filth from his face with the cool softness of her veil and was rewarded by the imprint of his image on the veil of her life; the trinity of Marys who kept vigil beneath the cross, courageous, while all the apostles but John hid in fear.

Proudly my mother related that it was to women that Jesus first made his resurrection known—to Mary of Magdala, to Mary the mother of James, and to Johanna. They were sent to proclaim his mystery, which the apostles thought was nonsense but which was, nevertheless, true. Finally, she spoke of Mary of Magdala's grieving in the garden over the loss of Jesus, whom she loved, how he appeared to her disguised as a gardener, and how she recognized him because she knew how to listen to his voice. Because of her love he made her the first apostle of the resurrection.

So I learned in the manner in which all the greatest mysteries are learned, through experience and story—woman passing on to woman, mother to daughter, those mysteries of power and meaning. She did not teach me theology or Scripture; she made no distinction between the literal and the symbolic; she told a story, and through it she gave me power. Even as a child I felt myself giving myself over to the story, reaching deep within myself to the reservoir of energy that would permit me to stand on the edge of life facing the death of everything. I wanted to be with those women. I wanted not to be afraid of the ebbing away of all that seemed most beautiful and loving in the world, but rather to stand there, to participate in the ebbing, to feel the release of that energy of life, to let go with him, to be faithful beyond human understanding. I accepted the story as power. I did not know until I knew Judith that my acceptance of it would make me dangerous.

What do women know that permits us, requires us, to stand courageously on the edge of death accepting it? Why do the Scriptures present us with the three Marys and the boy, John, standing on the threshold of such dangerous power while the leaders of the apostles—Peter and James—had fled?

Woman contains the life process—its beginning and ending, its flow and ebb—in her emptiness. She is earth-womb, birth bringer, life sustainer; she severs each cord, releasing life to a greater power. She, in whose emptiness life flows monthly most often into death, is no stranger to dying. She is more than she is. She knows each circle of life and death spiraling in cosmic creation.

In Jesus woman birthed her greatest son, who by his death and rising revealed her emptiness to be vastness and the fullness of power. She stood at his dying as trinity—virgin, bride, and mother—with the eternal son, the boy: "Woman, this is your son." Then to the disciple he said, "This is your mother" (John 19:26 JB). Not "Now, John, take good care of my old mom; she'll need protection when I'm gone," but a formal recognition of the identity of woman in her relationship to humankind as well as to the community of Jesus followers. Since John was the only representative of the male apostles present at the death of Jesus, he was, in the stead of them all, taken into the cosmic and creative emptiness contained within woman. He participated in that power, experienced that vastness, shared with her the death-severing implosion that transformed her vision of him to whom she had given birth into the vision of the Cosmic Christ.

The dying of Jesus happened in womanspace, as did his birth and rising. He is the prototype of humankind, she of woman-body/womansoul: the container of power, the bone weaver, the vast space in which and through which the Word of creation is spoken and enfleshed. Contrary to androcentric interpretation, she does not take her meaning from him; rather, she is a source of meaning in her self, as woman. She is, with him, the original priest: there can be no priesthood when they are separate, one from the other. She is ultimate. She contains the emptiness from which he springs forth. Out of her he lives, and into her he dies. Together they are the process of creation, the ebb and the flow.

She remembers the mysteries.

In his dying and rising Jesus becomes icon of the passageway. He opens all barriers to life, rending the veil of the temple of law, breaking open the sky to reveal its dark void, bursting through the sealed doors of the tomb. He opens again the way to feminine power. Contemplating this event, woman knows herself to be Cosmos—the holy space within which the mystery unfolds. She is the void within which death and resurrection bring forth a New Creation. She is earth opening to give birth to healed humanity.

Jesus is the Way. He is the passageway through her empti-ness, the New Creation. She is the space, the Mother, the cos-mos, he the process of coming to be. Together they accepted death—the New Woman and the New Man—and it made them dangerous, powerful, the beginning of a new cycle of life.

He is the Word, she the Voice; he is the Vision, she the Seer. Together woman and man offer the gift of the cycle of life in a priesthood of creative power.

CHAPTER 3

Descending into Womanbody

For two weeks in June the earth drank rain as it drizzled, poured, sprinkled, pelted from the sky. Everything began to smell wet. A musty scent drifted up from the basement; towels in the bathroom stayed damp from shower to shower. Attempting to elude the inevitable depression from seeping into the soul as the dampness seeped through everything, people began to make "rain jokes." The priest on Sunday quipped lamely, "Where's Noah when you need him!"

The day I began to write this chapter the rain had stopped. I relaxed on a lawn chair in the backyard, feeling the warm sun penetrating my skin and bringing me to a lazy awareness of my body. A mosquito-sized hornet flitted around my foot. It was so tiny as to be almost transparent, and sunlight shone through it, rainbowlike. It rested, poised on my toe; it was not even so heavy as the sunlight. Because the warm rain had stimulated their growth, the plants seemed giant. A rose stood straight and sturdy on a yard-high stem; I debated whether or not to cut it and bring it into the house. No. Better to come into *its* house in nature to enjoy it. A field of daisies dipped gently in the breeze. I carved another bite from the orange hollow of a melon and felt its cool sweetness in my mouth. In the house next door Jesse and Anna chattered and giggled over their noon lunch. I felt myself dissolving into the early summer earth and closed my eyes to enjoy the sensation. Before I dozed, a thought surfaced: For me, as woman, Jesus is not something to become but someone to bring forth. Jesus is the result of our descent into the body; we birth him in the release of our power—the new creation. The hint is earth. Incarnation.

When I went back into the house, I called Bethany.

After she left the religious community to which both of us belonged, I saw Bethany rarely. She was lost to me. I can count on my fingers the occasions on which we met, briefly and stiffly. We were afraid of one another, perhaps afraid of being caught again in the labyrinthine tunnel descending to darkness. Bethany had been my dearest friend during our novitiate years but had experienced an emotional collapse when we were away at college. It had been just the two of us. I remembered more about the details of her pain than she did. We felt an ambivalent mixture of love, hatred, and fear that threatened to destroy us both. Always afterward, looking into one another's eyes, guardedly relating events of our lives, the pull of mystery woven into the web of our mutual past was too much, and we fled from one another. Neither of us was aware that we had not completed the dark descent that we both were required to make individually, separately, simultaneously. Neither could we know that when we completed that journey we would embrace at last as sisters.

When she surfaced in 1983, she wrote me three letters and then called by phone. I was just completing the work on my first book and was not at all certain that I wanted to complicate my life with the pain that always seemed to accompany our engagement with one another. She continued to initiate telephone conversations, during which I remained guardedly responsive, remembering past experiences with her when brief engagement was followed by abrupt and lengthy separation.

It was my book that finally brought us together. The art proposed by the publisher did not communicate the strength I wanted. Taking refuge under the cloak of professional need, I called Bethany, who is an artist, to ask if she would be willing to critique the design. That afternoon, after not having seen one another for five years and not having really trusted one another for more than twenty, we met over lunch. In that meeting both of us, and our relationship, were healed.

That day in June she was quietly delighted. "Christin, the most wonderful thing happened. I was outside by the juniper tree when an enormous butterfly drifted by on the breeze. I thought it was a swallowtail butterfly, but I wasn't sure, so I said, 'Come back here,' quietly and gently. And it came! It circled in the breeze and lit on the branch not more than five inches from my face; opening its wings, it gave me at least twenty seconds to study each marking—so I would know it—before it joined the breeze again."

Bethany knows earth. In the deep places below conscious thought she has been like a seed, stripped, required to disintegrate in the moist darkness, allowed to die in the service of a transformed life. She dared to live the ancient way of initiation for women: descending to the abode of the dark Mother, stripping herself of all protective falseness, dying, becoming inert matter, waiting for the healing touch of the God of Earth to revive her as woman in herself. Embodied woman. Earthed woman. Incarnated woman. Now earth knows Bethany.

We always have been and still are opposites. But we each embrace the other as the shadow side of ourselves. She spins a story for when we are old. We will buy a cottage by the sea where earth, water, and sky mingle. There we will tell stories to one another and to the animals—butterflies and birds, squirrels, deer, and a friendly dog—of the grand adventure of life. And we will listen to the story creation recounts to us.

For creation is the Body of God.

Bethany recently wrote to me: "We are fully ourselves as a seed is fully itself from the beginning. Prayer: a robin sings. Is any living human listening to that particular robin at this particular moment? *I* am listening. I am loving.

"Prayer is our response to the continual movement or call of God. It is not always the same call, and we are not asked always to respond in the same way. Truth is everywhere. What matters is what are we being called to do at a certain moment.

"It is different for everyone.

"Sometimes it seems as if the voice becomes quieter and quieter through the years. It is so secret and rooted that who can ever find it to uproot it?"

There is a mystery that women must enter into if we are ever to become wholly ourselves and know God, as Bethany knows God. We need to find that secret, rooted place. We need to enter the mystery of descent.

We must descend individually and collectively—and we must eventually bring our brothers and fathers and spouses along. It is the descent of each woman to join womanbody with womansoul. It is the descent of humankind to the place where the essential feminine waits in darkness. It is the descent of the Christ to become earthed, fleshed.

Many women find a model of this descent in the ancient Sumerian myth of Inanna. She was a goddess of the country from which our ancient parents, Abraham and Sarah, were called into the Promise. Perhaps they brought into their new faith something real and truthful from their old.

THE MYTH OF DESCENT

The myth begins

From the Great Above she opened her ear to the Great Below.
From the Great Above the goddess opened her ear to the Great
  Below.
From the Great Above Inanna opened her ear to the Great Below.

My Lady abandoned heaven and earth to descend to the
  underworld.
Inanna abandoned heaven and earth to descend to the underworld.
She abandoned her office of holy priestess to descend to the
  underworld.[1]

In this translation of the myth, *Inanna: Queen of Heaven and Earth,* by Diane Wolkstein and Samuel Noah Kramer, we see the beginnings of feminine descent in the act of listening, of awareness of the depths, of attending to the unconscious. After the attending, the *intending*—the descent. "Inanna *opened her ear,*" the receptor of wisdom, to the great below.

First listening, then the recognition of presence—the moaning of Ereshkigal, queen of the underworld. She attends to the pain of the repressed and imprisoned feminine, and then intends herself toward her sister in the depths. Inanna, queen of heaven and earth, goddess of love and of the morning and evening star, abandons the sky and her priesthood of love to descend into earth, into darkness, into death.

At seven gates she is stripped of her divine attributes, the power to be who and what she is, and then kneels naked at the feet of Ereshkigal, who

Fastened on Inanna the eye of death.
She spoke against her the word of wrath.
She uttered against her the cry of guilt.

She struck her.

Inanna was turned into a corpse,
A piece of rotting meat,
And was hung from a hook on the wall.[2]

After three days, when Inanna has not returned, her faithful servant, Ninshubur, seeks aid. The only one in the Great Above willing and capable of helping is Enki, god of wisdom, god of water.

From under his fingernail Father Enki brought forth dirt.
He fashioned the dirt into a kurgarra, a creature neither male nor female.
From under the fingernail of his other hand he brought forth dirt.
He fashioned the dirt into a galatur, a creature neither male nor female.
He gave the food of life to the kurgarra.
He gave the water of life to the galatur.[3]

Then he sends them into the underworld. Being so small, they are able to pass through the gates unseen and on to the very throne of Ereshkigal, who loudly mourns in her pain. They climb into her ears and empathize with her. After some time, the empathy does its work, and she offers them a gift in gratitude for relief from pain.

They ask for the corpse of Inanna and sprinkle upon her the food and the water of life. She is reborn.

Because of her journey to the underworld, Inanna took on the powers and mysteries of death and rebirth, emerging not as only a sky or moon goddess but as the goddess who rules over the sky, the earth, and the underworld—as the Goddess in all her aspects.

Inanna becomes a metaphor for every woman who braves the journey into the deep places and who rises to a new and more whole life. As a symbol of feminine descent, she also becomes a promise that the pain we experience enduring the transformative process will not last forever. Instead, the food and water of life will be given to us freely. We will break through the pain and apparent certain death to greater being.

I suspect that everyone is called to descent sooner or later. I opened my ear to the Great Below in the years between 1968 and 1972—an experience that coincided with a struggle to decide whether or not I should leave the convent where I had been a Roman Catholic nun since 1958. We are often called to descent through dreams—and my process of leaving that way of life was initiated by my first dream of descent. It was a terrifying dream that haunted me during all the years that I struggled with decision about my life, and it did not finally lose its numinous quality for me until that decision was made.

All is dark, but wind blows within and outside of me—terrifying, evil, destructive. I must find the source of the wind. I seek Sister Marie, sister of the light and of the air, but she is not here. Sister Doreen, sister of earth, awaits me. "Come, Christin, to the wind's source. You must enter the place of its origin or be destroyed."

We take the road of darkness through the deep wood down to the center. As we approach the opening, the wind tears at me with such force that I feel I am being consumed. We turn a corner suddenly. At the center is a glass house filled. with light and with the demons who create the wind. Horrified, I scream, "Light". . . and I awake.

Years later, after I had emerged into a radically different kind of life—with a transformed awareness of myself, the world, and Holy Mystery—I experienced another descent dream, this one as much a blessing as the first seemed to be a curse.

A man stands up to his knees in clay in the center of the riverbed. He is a sculptor or a potter and is collecting clay for his craft. I am curious about what lives down the river and ask him. He replies, smiling, "Monsters. Prehistoric creatures. Danger."

Just then two women come to tell me that the girl-child I was caring for is lost. Running to the edge of the earth, I gaze over into the city below. There is a door opening into the city through which the girl-child may have gone, and a door at the edge of the earth that might lead to a passageway down. Going through the door at the edge of the earth, I find a stairway and begin to descend. I lose control of the descent as the tunnel becomes undulating and vaginal. All is darkness. I fear I am being swallowed up and will be lost forever in the center of the earth. At the height of my terror the tunnel curves and I slip out into an earth-colored room, which I know immediately is the private domain of the Great Mother Goddess.

Everything in the room focuses on her sacred table, which blocks the only door and prevents my escape. Instinctively I know that I must refrain from touching this symbol of her Mystery. The table is a mandala with arrows in a cross pointing to the four directions and containing the four powers of the universe. Suspended from infinity above the table is a silver sphere—magical, cosmic. I feel myself to be alive and dead simultaneously, confined to this small space and expanded to the limits of the cosmos. I reflect that nothing in my religious upbringing has prepared me for this and I must stand as an initiate awaiting the will of an intellectually foreign, but sensuously and intuitively intimate, divinity. Awesome energy, a feeling of expectancy and danger, begins to course through me as I gaze at the silver sphere and give myself over to the Goddess. As I begin to kneel at the table's edge, the door behind the table opens slowly and I am beckoned outside. Suddenly I know the girl-child has come this way and I will find her on the other side of the door.

I stand in a paradise at the center of the cosmos, within a sphere of green. As far as I can see, rolling fields of grass, trees, and flowers sparkle in sunlight. Homes for the inhabitants of this place are circular domes cushioned in the hills. As I catch my breath at the beauty, I see three women approaching me. I reach out my arms to them. When they are near, I ask, "Have you seen the girl-child?" but I know she is safe with them, and I relax into their presence as I awake.

For women, identified with the body by a dualistic culture that associates body with base instincts, the descent can be especially resisted in an effort to conform to the airy realm of the powerful and ruling patriarchy. By patriarchal standards a descent into the body would be to relinquish everything that patriarchal culture tells us will set us free. But such freedom is destructive and without grounding; it is a freedom from our very selves, a detachment from the source of our life and power. In

Descent to the Goddess, Silvia Brenton Perera writes of modern woman: "She must go down to meet her own instinctual beginnings, to find the face of the Great Goddess, and of herself before she was born to consciousness, into the matrix of transpersonal energies before they have been sorted out and rendered acceptable."[4]

We perceive a terrible danger when we are called to descend into womanbody, and it is not surprising that we do, for much of the spirituality we have been taught has emphasized this danger by labeling the body a burden, often evil, sometimes demonic. The spirituality into which I was initiated in the convent novitiate leaned decidedly toward a disembodied angelism, which would have destroyed me had the call of earth not been so intense and insistent through nature and the intimacy of the women and men I loved.

Filled with women though it may have been, religious community life during the time I participated in it was a part of the realm of the fathers. Leaving the convent became for me a descent to the Goddess, the elemental feminine within. The system of identity in which I had clothed myself as an adolescent girl needed dismembering. I let myself dismember in order to remember a self rooted in womanbody. It has taken me since 1968, and I suspect I am still engaged in the transformation today.

CHAPTER 4

Surviving Descent

Addie hears voices telling her to kill herself; they come in the night or day, unexpected, out of some great darkness Addie assumes is hell. Sleep brings no escape; the voices lure her even there, more terrifying because they are clothed in images she knows—grandmother, aunt, cousin—all dead themselves, presenting her with knives, guns, pills guaranteed to disembody her at last.

Addie is nineteen years old, but ancient in her experience of pain. Born to an unmarried adolescent girl, Addie was unwanted from the moment of her birth. Addie's task, from the beginning, seemed to be to atone for being born. One way of doing this was to stand in as mother to the brothers and sisters who continued to come until there were twelve, and to stand in as sexual partner to the man who began living with the family when she was eight. He was cruel, threatening Addie with death, denying he had ever harmed her when she reported the incest to the authorities, continuing to live with Addie's mother—battering her, laughing sardonically at Addie's concern, rolling the shells from his gun around in his hand while he watched Addie meaningfully out of the corner of his eye.

Addie was placed in intensive psychiatric therapy. Over a period of two years she has been out of the hospital for only short periods of time. While she is in the hospital, she worries about her mother and fights doctors who prescribe shock therapy, who prescribe medications for schizophrenia, for manic depression, for borderline personality disorder. When she goes home, her family urges her to use "crack" or to smoke marijuana, both of which bring on the "voices" with constantly increasing intensity.

She hides herself in flesh, two hundred pounds of barrier between her psyche and the world of pain. Then she starves herself because she hates her body so. In both the gorging and the starving she hopes Addie will disappear: Addie the ugly, Addie the unwanted, Addie the powerless, Addie who shouldn't be, Addie the raped, Addie the haunted, Addie who talks with the dead.

She who has been degraded now degrades herself. She who was denied from birth now denies herself the right to be.

None of us can predict how Addie's story will end or what process will lead her either to an act of power whereby she finally births herself or to an act of desperation ending in self-destruction. And Addie is not simply an example of woman's dilemma; Addie is real, alive and in pain. She is herself and she is all of us. What really happens to her affects each of us. And what we each do about rebirthing ourselves—descending into the body, encountering the dark Mystery, sacrificing our illusions of powerlessness, claiming our true and living power, and rising embodied and loving our embodied selves—creates or destroys ourselves and strengthens or diminishes Addie.

RESISTING DESCENT: DENIAL, DEGRADATION, DEATH

Here on the surface, confronted by the expectations of a patriarchal social structure, it is difficult not to deny a body that identifies us with earth and its spiral of production and decay. This is the cosmic process that masculine energy attempts to transcend in its linear thrust for increase and eternal life. We, women and men, deny the feminine energy of materiality in favor of the masculine energy of spirit. In so doing, we unground ourselves by denying all our embodiedness: the individual body, the earth body, the cosmic body, and, finally, even the Body of Christ. We become body haters both physically and symbolically, and unless we can let that hatred go and sink again into the primal matter of our embodied humanity, we will cease to exist as individuals, as earth, as cosmos, as Body of Christ.

As women we need to let go of our hatred of our bodies in

both their physical and symbolic manifestations. Why do we hate our physical bodies? First, our bodies do not conform. As I listen to myself and to the women I know, both as friends and as clients, I discover that we bemoan our failure to conform physically to some norm for appearance: breasts too small or too large or too drooping, hips too large or too small or out of proportion, waist not small enough, stomach too round, knees or ankles too big, buttocks too flat or too protruding, face too square or too long or too round, nose too big or too small, eyes too close together and not large enough, lashes not thick and long enough, lips too thin, ears not flat enough to the head, skin not clear enough or the right shade, hands and feet too big. By whose standards?

Shall we be the temptress or the angel? Are there any other choices? Perhaps the woman of the professional or business world. Each image has its form that we must fit. Conform. Temptress: long hair; wet red lips; curling, dark, extended lashes; off-the-shoulder shiny dress or tight black imitation-leather pants; 36-22-34; high-heeled silver sandals; low, breathy voice like the hiss of a panther. Angel: soft curls; a face exuding natural peace and gentleness; off-white cotton dress with a blue sash; sometimes pregnant, always virginal; modulated tones in a voice used for encouragement or consolation. Professional: hair pulled back with ivory combs and twisted into neatness; careful eyes; determined mouth and brow; pin-striped suit with a thin tie on a faintly feminine blouse, in colors permitted by color analysis codes; jewelry of sterling silver or pure gold; soft leather briefcase; low-toned and confident voice. Each image is 5' 7" tall and weighs 125 pounds.

Why do we conform? What would happen if we refused? What if we stood before our mirrors: "Mirror, mirror, on the wall . . ." and then not "Who's the fairest one of all?" according to some fickle standard, but "Who am I and what does this body need in order for me to be fair to me?" There is spirituality here, a reuniting with myself, an embracing of my body as expressive of my total being. How can I be fair? What style is most fair to my hair? Is makeup fair to my face? What clothes give fairness to my body? Are they warm or cool enough? Am I free to breathe, to move? Do the colors reflect my moods? Are my shoes fair to my feet and to the stance of my whole body? Am I comfortable? Com-fort: with strength, able to express the strength of my self through my embodiedness.

It may be that for many of us this contemplation of body—of *my* body, of the body that *is* me—could be the primary spiritual discipline. Perhaps the courage to be *comfortable*—able to be with my own strength—will, for many of us, constitute our initial act of power against a system that degrades us and teaches us to deny our womanbody in favor of a conformity that limits us to expressions useful only in the perpetuation of the anti-body system.

Though it may seem minimal, changing my appearance can be revolutionary! Some months ago I had occasion to hear a talk by a woman whose work was as a corporate executive for an international company. She demonstrated her transformation as a person within the confines of her job by changing her jacket at strategic points in the telling of her story. She started out with a manly charcoal gray to represent her attempt to establish herself in the system, moved to a severe black with strict lines as she told of her initiation into management with its strictures against interpersonal understanding, donned a beige tailored suit as she began to "come into her own," and ended in a coral-colored jacket designed for beauty, comfort, and freedom of movement as she brought her story to a close. She was on the verge of leaving the company to set up a business of her own with a system designed more along the lines of the coral-colored jacket. Coral became revolutionary alongside basic gray.

It is important to note that her transformation did not destroy her. Rather than conform, she transformed to be fair to herself and ended by expressing her self as fair. I have talked with many women who are convinced that they need to present themselves in a conforming manner or they will be disregarded. That may be true. We are so accustomed to imitation in our society that we often prefer it to what is real. The real is not regarded as suitable. Unsuitably presented, we should not be surprised if we are disregarded. As imitations we have been controlled and are controllable. An imitation takes the form it is given. It conforms. At times, to get a job, perhaps, we may find ourselves conforming, but we need to know that we weaken ourselves by so doing. We let go of something essential to our spirituality. We will not be *comfortable* in that act. As long as we acquiesce to our *discom-fort*—acting without strength in ourselves—we perpetuate our powerlessness.

A second reason we hate our bodies is that we cannot control them. My body will not obey me; it reflects the pain I want to hide, it disintegrates and dies. The betrayal here, however, is not on the part of the body. Instead, some part of me against nature—an unnatural part—rises up to assert its independence of creation. "I will not be subject to earth; I will rise above this common human lot and subject to myself this body of death!" Even Paul discovered the futility of such an act of pride when he cried out to heaven, "Who will rescue me from this body doomed to death?" (Romans 7:24 JB). And heaven's response: "My grace is enough for you" (2 Corinthians 12:9 JB). Is the grace Incarnation? I think so.

I was impressed by a client some weeks ago who, when telling me of some of her experiences of becoming physically ill during periods of emotional stress, compared her own experiences with a friends's. "She can't feel anything without her body being affected!"

I began to sympathize with the friend's dilemma, but my client cut me off.

"Oh, no, she's really fortunate. Imagine, to have such a sensitive, well-tuned body; she always knows when something is going on with her so she can deal with it. The body does not lie."

The body records our distress and plays it loud enough for our hearing. That may be the second most primal movement of our spirituality; after contemplating our appearance, we need to listen for the body's language.

Suzanne Swanson, an archetypal psychologist, and I spent a summer preparing through our own experiences to conduct a workshop for women called "Womanbody, Womansoul." We devised numerous activities we hoped would assist us and other women in healing the unnatural separation between mind and body, between body and soul. We hoped to activate the spirit or energy of bodysoul, which is only creative when we can realize our fundamental connectedness within and between. We worked with women whose disconnection had resulted in extraordinary pain. One felt nothing below her neck; another experienced herself as a starving, imprisoned woman, although she weighed over two hundred pounds; a third could barely speak above a whisper, although she held a professional position of considerable authority; yet another, whose spouse was a victim of suicide, felt paralyzed with grief. These four women and more like them tried—through dance, artistic expression, imagery, acting out dreams, and other activities done in an atmosphere of intense spiritual concentration—to make the reconnections within themselves, between themselves, to their world, and to the cosmos. Their attention to the body's language made possible the revelation of their souls.

I expect that our greatest hatred of the body arises out of our certainty that we will die. We who cannot fathom extinction say simply that our bodies die. It feels like a betrayal. My body cannot be me, because my body dies. If I accept my body as me, a bodysoul, then *I* die. But *I* am immortal, or will rise, or will be reincarnated. My body I discard, unimportant, to disintegrate.

I recall an argument with a professor of English in college. She was a gaunt, pale nun with piercing gray eyes whose every word commanded authority. It was over Gerard Manley Hopkins's poem "The Caged Skylark."

> As a dare-gale skylark scanted in a dull cage
> Man's mounting spirit in his bone-house, mean house, dwells—
> That bird beyond the remembering his free fells;
> This in drudgery, day-labouring-out life's age.
>
> Though aloft on turf or perch or poor low stage,
> Both sing sómetimes the sweetest, sweetest spells,
> Yet both droop deadly sometimes in their cells
> Or wring their barriers in bursts of fear or rage.
> Not that the sweet-fowl, song-fowl, needs no rest—
> Why, hear him hear him babble and drop down to his nest,
> But his own nest, wild nest, no prison.
>
> Man's spirit will be flesh-bound when found at best,
> But uncumbered: meadow-down is not distressed
> For a rainbow footing it nor he for his bónes rísen.[1]

She insisted that the poem meant we were caged by our bodies and longed to be rid of them for our spirit-song to soar to the heavens. I countered that the cage must be something other than the body itself. Rather, it must be a manner of *regarding* the body. It is our regard for the body that uncumbers us. Acceptance of the body as nest, wild nest, our own nest, is what makes it no prison. The body must not be distained; it will be everlasting. Risen.

She told me angrily that I was a heretic and was calling the good Jesuit one as well!

We are egocentric and do not understand the great round of women's spirituality, so we fear the death of the body. We fear earth, ungrounded as we are in this society, and so we fear to dissolve into earth. We think the earth is less than we are, and so we are humiliated to join it, to be loam, clay, to become the Great Body. But how else shall we learn wisdom? How else shall our "bones risen" rejoice in the connection of all life? I am myself, but not only myself.

> I have been in many shapes,
> Before I attained a congenial form.
> ....
> I have journeyed as an eagle.
> I have been a boat on the sea.
> ....
> I have been a sword in the hand.
> I have been a shield in the fight.
> I have been the string of a harp.
> Enchanted for a year
> In the foam of water.
> I have been a tree in a covert.
> There is nothing in which I have not been.[2]

Death is the dissolving into the Great Mother to await the Word of Creation, the brooding of the Spirit over the deep, which is her earth-womb. The body cannot be destroyed; it can only be dissolved into the larger body of earth. Distinctions I perceive are illusions. Everything is connected now in what I call "life" and will be closer connected later in what I experience as "death." There is nothing to fear. There is nothing in which we have not been. There is nothing in which we shall not be.

My life depends on my willingness to descend to the body. Cosmic life depends on the willingness of all of us, for in our prideful fear we have come far in destruction. Knowing we cannot destroy matter (*mater*, mother), we seek by force to bring it (her) under our control. We attempt to form earth to our will, to serve us. We want to leash her power so that we cannot be destroyed by it and so that we can use that power for destruction, even of earth herself. Much has been written, spoken, sung, chanted, sculpted, painted, to bring us to consciousness of the danger we are in from the manipulation of nuclear power, from the misuse of chemicals, from the rape of the land, from the pollution of the waters and air. Earth is our body and we do not respect her. We no longer consider her mysterious and holy. But if we murder her, we will all lose our life.

Woman is earth. She becomes symbol for all that humankind perceives as good or evil in earth-matter. At times in our human story that meant being held in honor as life giver, provider of nourishment, healer, spinner of life's thread, weaver of knowledge, lap of comfort, receiver of death. Respect for woman wanes directly in proportion to our lack of respect for earth. When we take control of earth, use it to our egocentric ends, waste it, disregard it, think of it as base, without spirit, inert, how will we then regard woman? Truly, we fear both. As women and as men, we fear womanpower, earthpower. We debase what we fear, keep it in its place, bury it deep beneath what we can control. And womanpower waits there, in our depths, to be released. Our only hope of survival is to descend.

THE SEVEN GATES OF DESCENT

Descending requires us to let go not only of a false self that threatens to destroy us but also of beauty and truth we have striven all our lives to envision and attain. Whether we have taken the path of the fathers, educating ourselves in their institutions, learning their language, seeking their goals, energizing ourselves with success in their endeavors, or supported the fathers in their path, creating their homes, birthing and rearing their children, encouraging their dreams, healing their wounds, we have most often made beauty out of our work. We rejoice in our careers and in our children. We are proud of our spouses' achievements and our belief that helped to make those achievements happen. For the most part, we understand our world, our place in it, our possibilities for advancement, how to achieve success.

Then one day everything is dry. Dust. Crumbled and blowing

away on a stale wind. Being vice-president of the company no longer matters. Being a competent wife feels meaningless. It is as though the house burned down, the cooled ashes stirred only by the footfalls of a ghostly self.

The time has come, not to reclaim what has been lost but to descend.

Perera suggests that the seven gates of the myth through which Inanna must pass might be analogous to the seven chakras of Hindu spirituality. The spiritual journey is usually perceived as upward. Teresa of Avila's seven mansions, each one higher than the one before, Thomas Merton's seven-story mountain—*up* to God. The chakras are no different; it is quite a revolution in thinking and experience to *descend* the chakras to find God rather than to *ascend* them. I suspect that we will find in our lives that true spirituality is both ascending and descending. To find the depth of God, however, we must descend—to find the ground of our own being we must descend.

THE FIRST GATE: THE GIVING OF THE CROWN

At the first gate of the descent I let go of my past, imperfect consciousness of God. Whatever that awareness may have been, I am asked to depend on it no more. What was once an image powerful enough to connect me to all being with what seemed a cosmic consciousness now is revealed as an idol. Either there is no God or God is so far deeper a Mystery than what up to now has formed my consciousness that I cannot any longer call this former beauty God. What I have known as God, a silver crown upon my head, a silver power connecting heaven with my earth, I now set aside. As I let go, all that I knew of God whirls away, silvering space with glory. Now no more mine. Each image by which I entered into union with the Holy, gone. Where once I was connected to the universe, where I played among the stars and danced on the face of the moon, where I walked forth on the rays of the sun, now will be only cosmic void. I see a lotus of a thousand petals shimmer momentarily and disappear. The universe is dark, and I am alone in a night with no moon.

THE SECOND GATE: THE GIVING OF THE EYE

At the second gate I am asked to surrender my inner sight and that unique light by which I envision the manifold connections within and integrate them into a unified "I." As I let go of my inner eye, all the illusions I have bound together reveal themselves, and the "I" fashioned over all the years crumbles and falls in the unbinding. Without this sight the eyes of others will be dark to me. The power to heal and the power to teach require seeing through pretense. All lies must be stripped away. After the unbinding, a multitude of faces rise to taunt me, each mine, each a stranger to me: mother, teacher, witch, fool, nun, lover, fairy child of the dark woods, betrayer of promises, priestess of the crystal cave, caldron woman, druid woman under the yew trees, beggar woman by the road, whore dying in her own blood in a squalid room, killer woman, knife woman, snake woman winding through the mysteries, bleached white man with sharp teeth, man without skin, small brown boy, lost, weeping child calling "father, mother," king man, warrior man, old woman weaving a basket, old tea woman, skull-faced woman crowned with thorns, mystic woman, song woman, woman with a mouth full of words, spirit woman. Unbound, I am their prey. After my giving of the eye, they accompany me in the descent.

THE THIRD GATE: THE GIVING OF THE OPEN THROAT

At the third gate all that passes into me as nourishment and all given out creatively I must let go. For what had nourished before, now seems poison, and what I have created seems a vessel made by another that holds no life for me. Words catch in the throat; my life is a whisper into the void. One by one the nourishers walk from the gate returning to the life I left behind in this descent. No longer can I depend on their gift: the mother's milk, the father's wise word, the friend's laughter and tears, the spouse's loving presence. I cannot receive now. I must learn the emptiness of no gift, of the closed throat. And I cannot give. There can be no lullaby for the child, no ballad for the lover or friend, no hymn for the hidden God. Receiving requires purity from selfishness—the gluttony of desiring my own fullness. Creation wants a free assent with no ties to my hunger for recognition. I cannot receive now, and I cannot give. The word has died in my throat; the song is silenced on my lips.

THE FOURTH GATE: THE GIVING OF HEART'S BREATH

How shall I pass through the fourth gate? I hold in my hands all the love I have known in my life, compassion for wee things reaching out to me, friendship with so many befriending me. It is the last of the upper gates; if I pass through, I could die. Breath catches at the intersection of heart and lungs and whirls with pain. I worry for their lives if I am not there to pour myself out to them in love. This is the gate at which I need to learn I am not necessary to the survival of the world, or of the wee ones I have tied myself to with my heart's breath. They will live if I let go of them. They will not suffocate if I let go of breath. The sigh of letting go is long at this gate. The gift is what I thought love meant, is my attachment to my care. I feel them, all the ones I thought I loved, whirling away, caught up in the breath of their own hearts. I am alone, descending into the lower regions—into fire.

THE FIFTH GATE: THE GIVING OF FIRE

This place is strange to me and fearsome. Power boils in caldrons almost running over. Solar gold shoots across the horizons of almost-consciousness, and I am gripped in an intensity of strength. The giving at this gate requires relinquishment of both submission and domination, of the illusion of control and the delusion of inferiority. When I have passed this gate, I will be neither over nor under any other, but beside in power. Competition overcome by combat: I am required to cast out games and become warrior. I let go of ease and take up the sword and shield of the goddess of war dynamic with a spirit of justice rising up from out of the earth. I let go my silence and receive the voice of those who cry in anger for a righted life. I scream and growl and roar like a she-bear rising, rising from the place of burial, from the place of forgottenness, from the place of fire. I am filled with fire. I ascend with fire as I descend past the fifth gate into the flow of water.

THE SIXTH GATE: THE GIFT OF WATER

At the sixth gate all that is rigid dissolves and flows into an immense living river; all that is one becomes permeable and flows into all that is other. Here I let go of the "sin of the flesh," feeling liquified and pulsing with life. Vulva, vagina, womb throb rhythmically like waves of an underground sea. I am the sea, vast womb of the world, container of mysteries, source of pleasure and life. I receive all that flows into and through me, and I let flow from me into the earth both the water and the blood. I let go the lie that I am not sacred. I ebb and flood; I let myself be tantalized by the moon; I reflect the sky. In the beginning was the deep, and darkness was upon its face. God plunged his Word into my depths and Light was made. I flow with the beginnings of all that is. I let go the lie that I am nothing. I am not nothing; I am the vast waters.

THE SEVENTH GATE: THE GIVING OF EARTH

I kneel naked at the feet of the Mother, knowing that the gift will be my life. All by which I have survived is forfeit. I must be remade. Her eyes blaze in the darkness and strike me with the look of death. Earth claims me. Black night engulfs me, thick, loamish, heavy, inescapable. Deeper than death I am buried in her, disintegrating within her, becoming part of her dark body. I am planted past all hope. Rooted. Dissolving like the seed, my former self decaying, becoming lost, becoming earth. Not even waiting, for waiting is waiting for something. There is no something. There is only earth. Being earth. The seasons pass over me. Leaves bud, flower, and fall curled and brown. Snow falls. Perhaps a year, perhaps twenty years. Who knows how much that was false there is to dissolve in me? Who knows when I will be conscious that I *am* earth? The mother waits; she knows. Life waits for me to don my body in awareness, humility, and pride. Earthbody. Bodysoul. Soulflow. Flowfire. Firebreath. Breathword. Wordvision. Visionlight. Lightcosmos. Cosmosgod. Godearth. Earthbody . . .

The descent spirals. We surface, finally, bringing the wisdom of the depths to the vision of the heights, allowing each to transform the other in the circle of life.

CHAPTER 5

Incarnation by Descent

There is a relationship between the experience of descent and the Christian mystery of Incarnation. I want to re-vision Incarnation in the light of descent. Maybe it won't be too difficult. After all, doesn't the ancient Nicene Creed state:

I believe in one Lord Jesus Christ, the only begotten Son of God. Born of the Father before all ages. God of God, Light of Light, true God of true God. Begotten, not made, being of one substance with the Father: by whom all things were made. Who for us men and for our salvation *came down from heaven.*

And was incarnate by the Holy Spirit of the Virgin Mary: and was made man.[1]

Incarnation by descent.

Compare the two hymns—the one from the myth of Inanna, the other from the early Christian church, recorded by the Apostle Paul:

From the Great Above the goddess opened her ear to the Great Below. . . .
Inanna abandoned heaven and earth to descend to the underworld.
She abandoned her office of holy priestess to descend to the underworld.[2]

> Although he was in the form of God,
> He did not deem equality with God
> Some thing to be grasped at.
> Rather he emptied himself
> and took the form a slave,
> being born in the likeness of men.
> (Phil. 2:6-7 NAB)

One evening in the summer, my spouse and I joined some friends for dinner at a local mall. After eating, we wandered through the arcade, in and out of little shops, admiring the cleverness and creativity of toymakers, dressmakers, toolmakers, when all at once Milly gasped, "Oh, Christin—look!" We were standing by an art gallery, and Milly was pointing at a poster print. In the center of the earth, under russet mountains, below white rock, in a cave or womb, sat a group of ancient women. Each of them held up a work of earth art—a woven blanket, a painting, pottery caldrons and bowls, baskets. All the colors of earth shone intensely at this enclosed center. I caught my breath: this print expressed in image everything I had been attempting to say in words. I felt a whirling in my own center, a joining of myself to the women in the earthwomb, a realization of the womanpower in which I shared. The inscription under the women seemed to be my own prayer, my own credo, my own offering:

> With that from the earth
> Beauty I will create
> With that Beauty
> My soul I will give.

I bought the print to celebrate Incarnation.

I have heard numerous arguments against the Christian mystery of Incarnation, its relationship to a feminine spirituality, and particularly its affect on women. The first and most often posed argument is that a religious image in which God is incarnated exclusively as a male cannot be helpful to women. How can women identify with such an image? If we do so, we always find ourselves in relationship only to a God that is other, never experiencing the ecstasy of loving the God within as she is revealed through our own womanbody, womansoul.

The second argument has to do with the materiality and historicity of Jesus of Nazareth, a fact that seems to take God out of the realm of limitless mystery and imagination and confine God to the historical reality of one man. Such confining also limits the religious imagination of his followers and threatens to identify certain real but disparate spiritual experiences and images as heretical. For example, women who believe their womanness to be not only an expression of God but an incarnation of that numinous Mystery, and who yet choose to be Christian, are faced with a radical spiritual, intellectual, and psychological struggle.

My own struggle for connection between my womanhood and my Christianity is by no means completed. I have, like the poet, only hints and guesses, musings that whisper through my soul. My convent experience hints. The poster print in the art gallery hints. Addie, listening to her voices of death, hints. I guess. "The hint half guessed, the gift half understood, is Incarnation."

My guess or my suspicion is that it is not that the Incarnation has limited us but that we have limited the Incarnation. We have *fixed* it like a butterfly on a collector's board, thinking to keep it, hold it still, study its components, distinguish its colors and design. Unfortunately, like the butterfly, the mystery has been almost killed by our attempts to *fix* it. Our main problem with the Incarnation is that, generally, we have literalized the Mystery and limited it to the historical person of Jesus of Nazareth. Because of our literalizing, our limiting, our fixing of Mystery, we run the risk of falsifying it altogether.

Just imagine for a moment that what we call Incarnation is not an event applicable only to the one person of Jesus at a distinct point in time. Imagine, instead, that Incarnation is a nonhistorical quality of the creative process of Ultimate God-Mystery that transfigures created being, radically shifts all consciousness in the cosmos, and results in what is earth-created matter becoming transformed into God. It is a quality of the creative process of God from the beginning, wholly present in the constant unfolding of created being, awaiting only the realization of creation itself in order to be manifest.

It is because Jesus *realizes* his radical Incarnation, through his conscious descent into embodiedness, that he is able to say, "Before Abraham ever was, I Am." (John 8:58 JB) He who was of the Great Above, like Inanna, opened his ear to the Great Below and emptied himself, taking a human (material, earth, body) form. What distinguishes Jesus from the rest of us is that he knew, was conscious of, who and what he was. He knew he was God's Word; that is not to say the rest of us are not. In one of his sermons, Meister Eckhart proclaims:

God becomes God where all creatures express God: There he becomes God. When I was still in the core, the soil, the stream, and the source of the Godhead, no one asked me where I wanted to go or what I was doing. There was no one there who might have put such a question to me. But when I flowed out from there, all creatures called out: "God!"[3]

The Godhead is the Source, the Numinous Mystery, the Divine Uncreated from which all being proceeds—from which the Word and the Image of God proceed. All that proceeds, all creation, *is* the Word and Image of God. All that proceeds *is* God. Descending into the Great Below, into the depths of creation and then ascending with the consciousness that creation is God is the meaning of Incarnation.

Everything that is created is God flowing from, having its source in, contained by the absolute ultimate infinity and otherness of the uncreated Godhead.

Incarnation unfolds towards cosmic consciousness. Jesus focused this consciousness within himself by fulfilling everything that is human, that is, by descending into matter, the Mother, the dark womb of the feminine and being born into the realization that he was God. By his own unfolding he became the Christ. The Christ is neither male nor female, Jew nor Gentile, slave nor free; the Christ is the fully incarnated one, the one containing in his or her consciousness the coming to be of all creation. And the Christ is God.

To be Christian means to enter into a process of incarnation. It means to descend as Jesus descended, to unfold as Jesus unfolded—not to become Jesus but to become ourselves so fully that we are Christ. We say he is the Way, not the destination. As women, we have a particular responsibility, for God incarnated in our being may add a dimension to cosmic consciousness, as well as to the Christ, that cannot be imagined in a creation expressed by a primarily masculine spirit. We have a responsibility to descend into, become one with, and then unfold the womanness of God in creation. That is how we become Christ. WomanChrist.

We need to ask ourselves, what am I? How can I come to enter fully into the creative process of my self? Just as Jesus allowed his bodysoul to completely manifest God, so also each of us women must allow her womanbody womansoul to manifest God. In this manifestation we are doing as Jesus did and consequently participating in the wholeness of Christ. We become WomanChrist.

As Paul proclaimed, Jesus, the Christ, is the firstborn of all creatures. It is not becoming Jesus that Christianity is all about; it is being born out of the depths of my human earth, conscious of the Christ I am. He is the firstborn. I must be born, now. You must be born. Finally, all of creation must be born into the consciousness of who and what it is: God, the Christ. That would be the fulfillment of both the Incarnation and the myth of descent. Paul said to the Roman community of early Christians:

Creation still retains the hope of being freed, like us, from its slavery to decadence, to enjoy the same freedom and glory as the children of God. From the beginning till now the entire creation, as we know, has been groaning in one great act of giving birth; and not only creation, but all of us who possess the first fruits of the Spirit, we too groan inwardly as we wait for our bodies to be set free.

(Romans 8:21-24 JB)

Doesn't that sound a bit like the groaning of Ereshkigal?

The intersection of the myth of descent with the mystery of Incarnation is the process of descending into our bodies (our physical bodies, our psychic bodies, our spiritual bodies, our cosmic body) and, through the touch of the Holy at the center, becoming incarnate God, just as the bodysoul of Jesus of Nazareth incarnated God.

Women represent the groaning of the feminine dimension of creation awaiting the glorious freedom of manifesting God in total consciousness. We need to descend through the seven gates, letting go of all that demeans, minimizes, and ostracizes us, and allowing ourselves, finally, to be the manifestation of God. WomanChrist.

Each woman is the image of God, just as each man is the image of God, but we have lost claim to our image. Where we have lost claim we now need to pro-claim. We need to speak what has not been said because it has been locked within us. Woman is the Word of God. We need to nurture the image of God within our essential creative void and let that image be born. Woman is the Womb of God. The power of incarnation is loose in creation; we must realize it in ourselves and be God-embodied. We need to reclaim our sister, the earth, so that the increasing of our consciousness will vibrate in her depths, so that air, ocean, ground, the round of seasons, the cycles of the universe will be accepted again as the flesh and the pulsations of the Holy God. Nothing natural can be outside the realm of our spirituality. Everything in the creative process is God seeking to be incarnated.

It can be done, will be done. Jesus is witness of that, for incarnation reached fullness in him. We must be as he, by giving ourselves up totally to the process of our own incarnation. Such is the meaning both of a feminine spirituality of descent and of Christianity.

The body into which we must descend to become incarnate is individual, communal, and cosmic. It is personal and collective. To become conscious of my self I need consciousness of God, and to be conscious of God I need to realize the connectedness of all creation. There can be no cry of pain in the world that is not my own. And not just human cries, but the cries of mountains being strip-mined and of streams being poisoned. There can be no violation of the Body that I do not feel as mine.

Incarnational consciousness demands descent to the body: my personal body, the body of my community, my earth, this cosmos. Not only do I need to unlock the Word and Image hidden in me, personally, and embody it; I need to be available for descent into that body of the human community represented by Addie and others like her—the energy of life or the forces of death. I need to realize my oneness with the mountains, the oceans, the prairie. I need to be awake to their vibrations within my own being. Descent is not only individual; it is also communal. Incarnation is cosmic.

So are you. So am I.

CHAPTER 6

Stranger of God

In August I went off by myself to a cottage bordering on a large nature preserve not far from St. Paul. Outside my window a meadow sloped down to a spring-fed pond surrounded by marshland, which was itself surrounded by hills of oak forest. The cottage sat on the side of a bowl of hills and meadows, with the pond and marsh at the center. A white egret made her home there and thrilled the air with her daily circling of the pond. She seemed the spirit of the place, a living white peace.

I had gone to this cottage for eight days alone with no agenda but to make myself available to the Mystery, the Holy One. Each day I walked the wilderness paths through woods, marsh, and meadow, sat at the top of the hill and sang to the egret atop her tree down in the marsh, let the silence seep into my soul, listened for the voice of the Holy, painted mandalas from images that appeared somewhere deep within me, wrote in my journal, watched the sun rise and set, let the darkness fall.

One day when I was wending my way down to the center to sit on the long footbridge that spanned the marsh, thinking about nothing in particular (looking back on it from this distance in time, I realize I was in harmony with all around me, hardly distinct from it), I heard a question deep within me: "If the Father God could not be whole enough for your worship and thereby betrayed your total trust, how will the Mother Goddess fare better?" Then the words "It is not enough!" I felt myself opening within to admit an image or inner vision. Yet that description is not precise enough. I felt myself to be one with creation, a brown, Buddha-like earth woman extending to the limits of the cosmos. At my center, within my womb, stood a masculine being of light and power, and I was bringing him to birth at the same time as he empowered my birthing. I knew then that I would reject the masculine side of myself or the masculine side of God at my own peril. Any attempt to discover the divine feminine leads us to uncover the divine masculine she encloses. The gift of the Goddess is that she discloses her enclosed Logos, Word of Creation. And that Word is "I am All."

A Jewish myth, told by a woman of the Minnesota Jewish community, relates that in the beginning God was both masculine and feminine. However, at a time close to, at, or just after creation there was a terrible cataclysm in heaven and the divine feminine became separated from the unity of the Godhead. Shekinah, the breath of God, the feminine, went into exile. The longing of God, the urgent yearning of all creation, ever has been and continues to be the reunion of what has been separated. Elie Wiesel reflects: "Exile envelops God Himself; God Himself is in exile. Language is in exile. The *Shekinah*, of course, is supposed to be everywhere, and it is exile that carries it everywhere. So exile for us is something which is as absolute, as infinite, as life."[1]

That yearning for reunion of what has been in exile persists in the living history of humankind, but in men and women differently. It is said in the myth that through the centuries, in many lands, men have met the Shekinah on the roads of their life journeys. One meets her as a beggar woman, another as a queen, another as a mother, another as an ancient crone. But it is not told that she has been met by any woman. Rather, women reveal her, are the veil for her, experience her exile in living out their lives. Each morning the Orthodox Jewish male prays that the Shekinah be reunited with the Godhead. Is he aware that this prayer could bring about in him a realization of Shekinah's presence in the flesh-and-blood women with whom he lives each day, and a development of mutuality with them? Perhaps the secret is that the divine reunion depends on the human one. Daughters, arise! Sons, be aware! The days of exile must pass away; the time of homecoming has arrived.

Because of the pervasive masculinization of culture that has increased and persisted for thousands of centuries in almost every part of the world, we do—women and men alike—suffer from a lost and alienated feminine. In fact, from the perspective of "soul" we hardly know what the feminine experience is, so when we are told that the soul is always feminine whether in men or women, we feel confused. Is the soul, then, passive, a stranger, hidden, something to be ravished, not powerful? We perceive the soul through masculine eyes; we see ourselves with masculine eyes. Masculine is power; feminine is the "other." If I am a man, it is dangerous for me to act from my "soul," lest I be seen as alien and powerless. If I am a woman and believe in the cultural connotations of the feminine, I will be oppressed; if I seek to change those connotations, I will be called "radical," "crazy bitch," "masculine woman," "troublemaker," "castrater," and other less printable names.

Fortunately, the Mystery we call God, who is the source of masculine and feminine energy equally, cannot be overcome by our distortions. Our oppressions of one another have, however, succeeded in blocking the passageways within us to the full expression of that energy in our lives. We now have only hints of the wonder of masculine and feminine in each of us and in the whole community of humankind. If this order of being we call our world is to be saved from our own destructive powers, we must find ourselves; to do that we need to rediscover Ultimate Mystery and undistorted masculine/feminine energy. We do have hints, like the "I Am All" image I spoke of earlier. We need to believe in those hints and allow them to grow in power.

Much feminist literature gives the impression that a masculine God, "God the Father," feels oppressive to every woman whose consciousness has been raised. The assumption seems to be that in a culture where masculine power has oppressed females economically, sexually, professionally, in the arts and sciences, in the family and at the club, in politics and religion—in that culure women would reject all that is masculine, not only in the culture but in themselves and in God as well.

A speaker and workshop leader at a women's clergy conference, a woman who is a nationally known author of books on biblical images of the feminine, admitted during her workshop that her work was on behalf of her "sisters" in the women's movement for whom reference to a masculine God was offensive. For herself, a woman whose own father was tender, loving, and supportive of her, the image of "God the Father" had always brought forth the deepest religious experience. Conversely, the

Goddess, or "God the Mother," caused inner turmoil because of her lifelong struggle to understand and resolve the tension between her own mother and herself. Many of the more than forty women in the workshop nodded their heads; some of them related their own difficulties with "God the Mother" and seemed to demonstrate both empathy and relief at having "God the Father" returned to them in a community of women most of us had expected would be "beyond God the Father."

So we find ourselves in a painful dilemma. As a people in this world we have so distorted ourselves as human beings that we have set masculine and feminine in a destructive relationship to one another. As a consequence, we no longer have a clear understanding of the masculine and feminine energies creatively active within each of us, man or woman, and in the whole cosmic order. Individuals identify with one energy or the other and suppress its opposite. Within us the Shekinah is exiled in the terrible psychic-spiritual cataclysm, and we are each either exiled to the land of otherness with her or condemned to seek her all our lives. Organized Western religion has limited God to the masculine, and it is not because "he" is masculine that we suffer but because "he" is limited.

I know of no creation myth that does not begin either with two elemental forces combining to produce all things or, more commonly, with an original One whose first act separates being into two dynamically potent forces. This original One is mythically represented as containing masculine and feminine as balanced, interpenetrating dimensions of its being. Words, however, are imprecise when attempting to describe as One forces we typically experience as opposites. There are no dimensions to oneness. There really is no way for oneness to divide. The myths attempt to express the imponderable—for without the division of the One into complementary energies, there can be no resultant creation of the many. So, inherent in the creative process is the distinction and interpenetration of energies that, though opposites, can never exist separately. We have, then, the mystery of the two that are really One.

We are limited by our limited image of God. The ongoing creation of the world is limited, perhaps even distorted, by our interior fragmentation. A society that insists on maintaining the power of one of the world's primal creative energies over the other will eventually destroy itself. Masculine energy developed at the expense of feminine energy results in an ungrounded culture, out of touch with the sources and repositories of life and vitality. Feminine energy developed at the expense of the masculine could result in a culture lacking in focus, direction, and brilliance. For creation we need both the clay and the breath of life, the vast waters and the spirit moving over them.

Not only does the society require the union of feminine and masculine energy; the individual needs that union in herself or himself as well. I am woman. I am earth. I am the void. I am darkness and the vast waters within which stirs that which will come to birth. I surround all that is—I surround the light. I surround the masculine; I form him; I feel his power coming to be in me; I am shaken by his sharp power. In the center of me his power becomes light, and the light becomes a word that I speak to create my world. He and I are one. I am woman: she who contains the masculine.

He who faces me in this world is man. He is rooted in the feminine, grows out of the feminine, reroots himself in her ground to become creative. Surrounded by her, he can include all life in his striving, be broad rather than narrow in his vision, tempered in his power. He cocoons himself in the feminine and transforms. The feminine becomes the mysterious alchemical environment within which man's transmutation occurs. Within her darkness he comes to feel upon and within him the awesome and slow process that takes him by the essence to work its alchemy. There is no escape from her vast, pulsing being, which turns his base metal into gold, his pitiless striving into tender love. He and the feminine are one. He is man: feminine-grounded power.

Our typical mistake when thinking about masculine and feminine energies in creation is literalization. We tend to associate masculine exclusively with men and feminine exclusively with women. Even though we may have read, and may even believe, that real men and women experience both masculine and feminine energies within themselves, or that in every man and woman flows a continuum of masculine and feminine energy and that the most mature person experiences a union of both in his or her living, we need to be reminded again and again. Women often react strongly against identification with only those energies designated as feminine. But they will bristle with equal indignation on hearing themselves called "masculine women." Many men claim that the traditional "feminine" characteristics are naturally part of their characters, but they do not want to be called "feminine men." This dilemma of people's fear of being identified with the characteristics of the other sex has led many, particularly in the women's movement, to eliminate sex differentiation from these primal energies and simply to call all of them "human" qualities.

This undifferentiation seems to me to beg the question. Clients report an actual psychic and spiritual struggle taking place within them between forces of their being they themselves experience as masculine and others they experience as feminine. These masculine and feminine dimensions of a person's being certainly cannot be understood simply when they appear as multifacetedly complex as a cast of Greek gods and goddesses.

Both the feminine and masculine energies are mythologized in these goddesses and gods as they are present in both men and women. The myths show us how superficial we would be to attribute some qualities entirely to men and some to women: for example, to say that men are powerful and women are loving. The myths teach us that there is masculine power and feminine power. Hercules may be powerful, but so is Hera, so is Artemis, so is Gaia. Aphrodite loves, but so does Eros. Power, love, or any of the human energies are full in us only insofar as we have realized within ourselves both their masculine and feminine sides. Although it is true that "masculine" and "feminine" are themselves metaphors just as much as are the gods and goddesses, they *are* helpful metaphors for our task of inner differentiation. Through that differentiation we can better understand the multidimensionality of our selves, experience the rich complexities of our human natures, and live richer lives.

The more of both the masculine and feminine energies I have accepted within myself, the more fully human I will be, but if I am to be true to my self, I will express those energies *as a woman*. I will express the masculine side of myself in a feminine manner. A man will express the feminine side of himself in a masculine manner. To pretend that being a women is not *different* from being a man is folly.

Women, however, in their personal, professional, and spiritual lives, encounter an overwhelming obstacle to their essential creativity in the masculinization of society. Seeking survival, some women have buckled under and become daughters of the fathers either by outdoing men in their masculine-toned achievements or, trivializing the feminine, by remaining daddy's little girl all their lives. In the first survival attempt, we identify with the masculine and imprison the feminine energy in our deepest unconscious; in the second, we project our masculine energy on our men (fathers, spouses, employers) and withdraw from the feminine and all of its power. That power then retreats to the unconscious. In our attempts to survive in a masculine world by denying the feminine, we succeed only in making ourselves powerless.

But the powerlessness extends beyond ourselves. In our withdrawal men, too, are drained of essential power. With only a caricature of woman with whom to relate, men become a caricature of themselves. Where is the strong, vibrant woman who calls forth the strong, vibrant man to engage together in an act creating the cosmos? Thoughtful men as well as thoughtful women are trying to find the selves they lost when we repressed our feminine energy.

The notion that masculine power is violent, abusive, egocentric, and dominating is simply wrong, although those characteristics seem to come easily to men who have been deprived of true feminine energy both within themselves and in the real women to whom they relate. We do not want men to become caricatures of the feminine—soft, submissive, pliant, and docile—any more than we, as women, want to be identified with those caricatures ourselves.

Some men, in attempts at liberation from masculine caricatures, seem to strive to reform their characters according to what they mistakenly think to be a feminine dimension. They end up being quite "nice," never angry, amazingly tolerant, gentle-eyed, soft-spoken, boring individuals. They lack the verve, the spark, the wildness, the rough-hewn quality, the diamond brilliance of essential masculine energy. Such masculinity has no fear of the feminine, does not need to repress her, does not seek to dominate her, but relates to her in a powerful, mutual, orgasmic intercourse of the soul that transforms us into whole men and whole women in the ongoing creation of the world.

Just as women in our time join together to uncover the buried feminine, to raise her again to our consciousness, to make her power available to our world, so men are beginning to make journeys into the wilderness to develop the embryonic masculine. They seek to call forth their courage in a life-giving struggle with nature rather than a death-dealing battle in war. They try to reclaim rites of passage into manhood not connected with drugs, violence, or sexual exploitation. They are beginning to tell their stories, raise their most feared feelings, bond with one another in true brotherly love.

Perhaps it is not so much the masculinization of society that has harmed us but the caricaturization of society. We need deepening. We need the rich ground and blazing sky of reality.

Our dualistic thinking has led not only to the characterization of masculine and feminine, but also to limitations and divisions of people based upon race and color. Simply put, in the dualistic scheme of things everything must be categorized as positive or negative, good or bad. If light is good, its opposite—darkness, or shadow—must be bad. The masculine that participates in the light principle is judged good, while the feminine as its opposite is bad. If white is good, black is bad.

A dualistic culture invests great energy in empowering the "good" and overcoming the "bad." In a white male culture, a woman of color becomes symbolic of all that is strange, all that is opposite, all that is feared and to be overcome. In a patriarchal religious system that imagines God to be a powerful white male father figure, the beautiful Black Goddess of earth, the Mother birthing creation, becomes a stranger to the Divine.

Each of us, woman or man, person of color or white, contains in our soul the image and power of the Black Goddess. For me as a white woman she represents that dark well of creativity as yet untapped but wherein lies my most profound truth. For a woman of color the Black Goddess may represent that awesome and sacred power at the center of her identity making her dangerous and necessary to the very culture that would keep her down.

The Black Goddess is rising in the soul of the world. Each of us, depending on how well we have been able to reconcile the opposites within ourself, or between the self and the culture, either fears her or welcomes her.

When she begins to rise, she shows herself in many forms: earth goddess, avenger/destroyer, black madonna, panther woman, queen. Encountering her can be terrible and marvelous. Although I have met her often in dreams—mostly in frightening ways—during the writing of this chapter she initiated me into the wisdom of my connections with her and the mystery of her identity for me.

In a dream a black infant girl struggles for her life. She weighs less than a pound and fits in the palm of my hand. I, too, am a black woman and have some relationship to this newly born child. Another black woman is singing in an adjoining concert hall; her mother is also a singer and I am somehow both the mother and the daughter. When she leaves the concert, I am amazed by her beauty: ebony black, with piercing eyes, dressed in rich and vividly colored clothes—blood red, indigo, silver, gold—and crowned with jewels. I call to her, and she and I walk together down the stairs. During this descent, she reveals to me all the connections, tracing my lineage through her, her mother, and thousands of black women to the first of all black women, who is somehow also the infant, who was a slave and whose name is Stranger of God.

When I awoke I felt filled with energy—feminine energy released from slavery—still fragile as the dream infant, but alive, born from the depths. I also knew that the name did not mean a stranger *to* God but rather the part of God that has been a stranger to us. She, the dark feminine, the essential woman, is God as Stranger, Shekinah—the God we do not recognize but is. I loved her in my self and my self in her. I loved her deeper than my self can reach, and I lost my self in her. I welcomed the Stranger of God and felt welcomed in my own birthing.

The dream collapses the continuity of time into present simultaneity and the differentiation of being into oneness. All of history presents itself in the descent to the beginning, and all women participate in the infant who is also the original Stranger of God. The dream has the character of creation myth. It takes place *in illio tempore,* in the beginning, once upon a time. We understand, from the time we are children, that these words indicate not so much a historical time as a state of being in an eternal present. The "beginning" we sense in mythological language or in the language of dream is also the deepest reality of the present and the fullness of the end. It is the state of being before division, when being was one, before the multiplicity of creation.

There can be no creation without the Stranger of God. Perhaps now, in our time, that creative power of energy, without which our world will become stagnant and sterile or chaotic and out of control, is the power symbolized by the dark feminine. So long as she is enslaved, or insofar as she remains enslaved, the creative dynamic will be impotent, for exile will continue to envelop the Holy One.

CHAPTER 7

Conceiving Creation

The manner in which a creation myth is told depends on the cultural perception of masculine and feminine power. In matrifocal cultures predating the rise of patriarchy, the original One was represented as the Goddess of All Things, who, however, contained within herself the fullness of masculine energy to which she gave birth and who became her opposite and creative consort God. Together they brought forth the multiplicity of creation. June Singer reconstructs one of these Goddess myths in her book *Androgyny*.

In the beginning the Goddess of All Things, Eurynome, rose naked from Chaos. Finding nothing substantial for her feet to rest upon she made a separation between the sea and the sky, and danced lonely upon the waves. As she danced toward the South she set the wind in motion behind her; then she felt the north wind and took it between her hands and rubbed it, and there was the great serpent, Ophion. Eurynome danced more and more wildly to warm herself, and Ophion grew lustful to see her and coiled himself about her limbs and coupled with her. This is the same north wind, also called Boreas, who is said to fertilize, which is why it is said that mares often turn their hindquarters to the wind and breed foals without the aid of a stallion. So Eurynome likewise became pregnant.

It is said that she then assumed the form of a dove, brooding on the waves. When the time was right, she laid the universal egg. Ophion the serpent coiled himself seven times around it, and remained there until it hatched and split into two parts. Out spilled all the things that exist, the children of Eurynome: the sun, moon, planets and stars, the earth and all that grows upon it.[1]

The Judeo-Christian creation myth articulated, out of a patriarchal worldview, a response to the fundamental question "Who am I and what are my origins?" The original One is a God rather than a Goddess, and creation results from Wording rather than from Birthing. Nevertheless, many of the mythic elements are similar.

In the beginning was chaos or nothingness, and the Spirit of God (Eurynome's dove) brooded over the vast waters. Then God spoke (the Word): "Let there be." The separations begin—first darkness from light and evening from morning, then water above and below the firmament, and finally woman and man from the human *one*. "God created man in the image of himself, in the image of God he created him; male and female he created them" (Gen. 1:27 JB). To be in the image of God is to be male *and* female.

Perhaps the story of creation in God's image is a way of attempting to articulate the inexplicable by means of metaphor. The Original One, essentially a union of what we know as masculine and feminine energy, demonstrated the essential creative tension between opposites by creating this Adam and this Eve in the likeness of divine essence. In the flow of oneness to separation to oneness again, which we witness in the man/woman metaphor, opposites differentiate themselves but remain held in creative tension by their original oneness. At each joining something new arises—a furthering of the multiplicity of creation flowing out, expanding the cosmic boundaries.

Dualism denies the Original One by its assumption that one of the opposites needs to give way in order that the other might be all-powerful. Often the one chosen to give way becomes designated as evil, to be avoided, fought against, repressed, killed. As the side designated as good detaches more and more, losing its original connection with its opposite, it loses its creative energy, becomes trivial, and finally is only a caricature of life, no longer in the image of God. God, before whom we are struck with awe, in the presence of whom we can only adore, becomes the Stranger, lost to us, hidden in what we have denied and repudiated.

Such is also the process by which we become strangers to ourselves and to one another.

So many of the women and men I see in spiritual direction

claim to be "looking for themselves." They feel an emptiness within, where the self is imagined to be. God, too, is lost or silent, imagined to be outside of them.

For women, both the lost self and the silent God seem connected to the feminine. One woman, a successful professional minister in a Protestant denomination, wept at the depth of her loss. All her life she had done the right things—she had organized her experience to make meaning out of it; she had been teacher and healer and spiritual advisor to many—but she felt hollow and silent within.

"I don't know how to be a woman," she wept. "The feminine part of life feels so foreign—everything I am not: earthy, creatively circular in thought, gentle, not needing a predetermined outcome, sensuously lovely, touchable, pliable, warm, and close. I am so jealous of women who can be like that. I never could.

"People have never liked me—I think it was because I couldn't be that way. People think I am hard, immovable, unfeeling. People think I can't be hurt, that I am powerful, able to endure anything. I don't know what I am. I don't want to give up what I am, and yet I want all that I seem not to be besides."

This woman had developed the masculine energies in herself at the expense of the feminine in order to survive in a religious and secular world where to be successful meant to be able to operate capably within a masculine structure of meaning and activity. All sanctions and all rewards for professional endeavors depend on being able and willing to think and behave according to a masculine model or, worse, according to a caricature of a masculine model. For such a woman to tap into her feminine energy, she would need to be willing to risk having her whole professional world fall apart.

Before the opposites can be reunited, the feminine must be raised. In many of us she has been buried so deep that the place where she is seems but an emptiness, a vast darkness, an infinite void. To give way to her is to slip off the edge of the known and plunge headlong into unknowing. It is to let go of organization and control and be whirled into chaos. Women daring this process of finding their essential selves have told me that it is a kind of "going crazy."

"I became an animal. I tore my hair and screamed. I climbed

into my closet and lay like a fetus in a corner sobbing and sobbing while the clothes hung around me, touching me like gauze
about to swaddle something newborn."

"I awoke in the middle of the night engulfed by darkness
and feeling the boundaries of myself give way to nothingness.
I was trembling and sobbing and my husband woke up—I
pleaded with him to hold me before I fragmented completely.
His arms seemed to permit a release within me of something
fearsome: a woman at the center of the earth, a woman in the
dirt and crying out and tearing at her hair, and her voice was
mine."

Women who dare to release the Stranger of God within themselves are becoming prophets to the world.

How are we prophets? We, women, are the voice for the
Stranger of God. We dream the Divine Feminine and are made
messengers for her. We become the earth in which she has been
buried and from which she is now ripping her way forth through
our bodies, through our minds, and through our feelings. She
comes forth in us out of darkness where she has been buried so
long she can no longer remember the name of her Child. She
no longer knows the Father, so long have the opposites been
torn asunder and the feminine cast down. She does not even
know that she comes to heal the dualism, so we do not know
either, the meaning of her coming—but she comes.

Our coming forth is hers. Our cries are hers. Our poverty is
hers. The labor in which we are involved is a labor to heal God
as well as ourselves. It is a labor without which the world will
come apart so far it will destroy itself. We will probably not understand our prophesy. If we learn its meaning at all it will be
in the whispers of our children as revealed by Gertrud Kolmar's
poem "Out of Darkness."

And now I stumble forward on the stony, stubborn path.
Jumbled rocks and thistles wound my groping hands:
A cave awaits me
That conceals inside its deepest crack the bronze-green, nameless
    raven.
I will enter
And crouch down to rest beneath the sheltering shadows of his
    giant wings,
And listen, drowsing, to the silent, growing word my child speaks,

And sleep, my brow turned eastward,
'Til the dawn.[2]

The cave to which we must return through the shambles left in the wake of dualism is the secret that women contain. This is the cave in which, covered by the wings of seeming death, we conceive the future in the image of a Child and then rest, awaiting the dawn. The ongoing creation proceeding from the cosmic, feminine cave comes forth as both Word and Child. The result is androgynous, a union of opposites, a synthesis of dualities. In the rest before the dawn the Child whispers of the future, becomes the Word, the Image of our hope, and we are saved by what we bring forth.

A woman's spirituality requires conception. So we must discover the cave within us as well as the cosmic cave constellated by a focusing of feminine energy universally. Physical conception by which a new human being is formed is but one dimension of this complex power through which feminine and masculine energies join in a creative synthesis. We also conceive images, individually and collectively, out of which flows new future for ourselves, our societies, our world. All conception requires a transcendence of dualism at the particular level on which it takes place: physical, imaginal, intellectual, social, spiritual. The masculine and the feminine must join in a creative synthesis—and that means the *real* masculine and feminine, not some ragged caricature of one, the other, or both.

In physical conception the joining is obvious: masculine sperm with feminine ovum to create the new, the embryo, which is, at least in the beginning, physically both masculine and feminine. But masculine and feminine energies transcend men and women. A women's group that lacks masculine energy cannot be creative. Nor can a men's group that lacks feminine energy. Creation depends on the synthesis. Even the process of individual growth depends on the synthesis. Relationships between two individuals depend on the synthesis.

One marriage therapist I know bases all his work with couples on the theory that for marriages to survive and become centers for human growth and transformation the man and woman must create a third entity beyond themselves. And they must continue in this creative process for as long as the marriage lasts. At first this third entity might be a child, perhaps a series of children, but finally the creative process must reach beyond childbearing and child rearing. Something in the interchange between the individuals in the marriage needs, constantly and consistently, to bring forth the new: new ideas, new projects, new levels of awareness—an art, a more humane social structure, a healthy and productive land, and on and on, limited only by the depth of people's willingness to give themselves to one another. Then that which we conceive together returns to us the image of who we are. It is not so much by looking inward that we find ourselves but rather by listening to the creation we bring forth.

It is no wonder we are poverty stricken in our selves and in our relationships. Often the limit of our creation is the purchase of a new commodity. We are buried in things. New things. The newest fashion in clothes, in household furnishings, in cars, in food, in adult toys. Together we create a new deck in the backyard, a new arrangement for the living room, a new look in the kitchen, a new garage to hold the new second or third car. Then we look to our things to tell us who we are. They break, they go out of fashion quickly and are disdained as old, they pile up and clutter our lives, they demand our time. We cast them aside, have a garage sale and buy something new. If what we have created together is so transitory, how can it carry the image of what we really are?

The more we seek in things for our selves, the more empty we become. We become trivial. Our relationships become more trivial yet. Finally, we are caricatures of men and women, and our marriages fails. We have created nothing worthy of us.

This spirituality of conception is nothing less than the revisioning and reconstructing of society. If the woman-cave is real, it can receive only an authentic masculine energy. The trivialized masculine will be sloughed off, bled out, discarded. But that which will be brought forth from an authentic, real conception will have the power and substance to whisper back to us the secret of who we really are. And I suspect that that secret contains hints of the ancient creation myths, that we are images of God, that we continue the Wording, the Birthing begun by the Original One, that we Mother and Father God in the world.

CHAPTER 8

Birthing Cosmos

Twice a month twenty women come to Widsom House to create new rituals. We have committed ourselves to one another to increase awareness of our experience as women, to mutually and honestly explore our Christian roots, and to re-vision and reconstruct our Christian worship in the light of our experience. We meet in a basement room—grounded, under ground—that has been designed to express an environment of earth. Thick brown carpeting, dark ceiling with indirect lighting, and rust-colored cushions create an enclosure for sacred space that is cavelike, womblike.

In November, when nature strips herself and darkness settles in, we chose to celebrate woman as birthgiver. Making a living circle of women in the darkness of our womb-room, we lit four candles, saying:

> Let us bring together darkness with light
> Celebrating the holiness of each;
> Let us become aware of the holy dark space within,
> The birth space,
> And of the light we bring forth.

In the flickering candlelight Kathy Callaghan led us in her meditation. "Let us close our eyes. I invite you to come with me on a journey, inward and outward.

"As we begin the journey inward, let us concentrate on our breathing. As the breath, the energy, goes inward, feel it touch different parts of your body. Feel the energy of the different parts; as you exhale, let go of what is unnecessary, taking no more than what you need.

"As you continue to breathe, search with each breath, search your own body, search until you come to a special spot, a place that you find within yourself, the place that is most receptive, the place most able to nurture. With your breath, fill that place; with the energy of your breath, leave the spark of life there. Be filled with energy. As you focus on your spot, remember that it is a unique spark, the spark that is you, the spark of creation that has never been before and will never be again. As you focus your energy on that spot, relish it, celebrate it. And from that deeply nurturing place, view the rest of your body, yourself. As you look at your own body parts, see if there is any part that feels lonely, unloved, discounted. Gently take those fragments and weave them with the power of your spark, taking time to weave those fragments into a unity. As you feel yourself becoming one within yourself, become aware of a journey outward. The nurturing spot is a womb, a safe place, like an island, a homeland. But birthing demands a crossing, and each journey is difficult; some have storms, fears, pain, nothingness. The destination is a place of new life and new freedom. There are many crossings back and forth, and each time the womb, the homeland, is changed. Each time the journey is different. Each time the destination, the birth, is a new beginning.

"I invite you to reflect, remembering a specific time, a time you birthed in that very core of your being. A time that showed you that you are holy in body, holy in birthing, holy in your womanhood. Take the time to remember, to nourish, to celebrate. . . ."

After some time of silent reflection, each woman shared birthing experiences through poetry, art, song, or storytelling. "On the day of my birth, God danced," said one. "A rose bloomed in our yard the day my daughter was born; we picked it on the way to the hospital, and although it was without water all during my labor, it lived to greet her birth, and then for days and days afterwards. Tonight, I give each of you a rose," another said gently. One woman told of her pain at never having birthed a physical child, another of the birthgiving involved in adoption. A nun spoke movingly of birthing her self. On and on around the circle women offered stories, poetry, and song. In the end we created a womb of our group, enclosing each woman whose birthday was in November and bringing her forth anew:

"Together we are woman—the womb of creation.

"Let us be that for one another tonight.

"Let each person born in November be birthed by us. We will form a circle, a womb, around her—create the passage to life with our hands—and welcome her into life with a new name, one we will hear mysteriously in our souls. . . ."

And then, ritualistically gathered, we chanted:

> "We are woman
> We are birthing woman
> We give life.
>
> From our labor
> We call you forth.
> As we give birth to you tonight,
> May you birth each of us in your time.
>
> As in the beginning
> We heard the Holy One call us each by name,
> So now may you come forth
> To the name by which you are called
> In each of our hearts."

There was a moment of intense silence. Then the names began to be spoken gently into the circle of women: I name you Deep; I name you Courageous One; I name you Dancer; I name you Shining One; I name you Dragonfly; I name you Joyful Youth; I name you Piney Wood; I name you Beauty; I name you New Woman; I name you Melody; I name you Gentle Lady; I name you Soft Rain; I name you Burnished Gemstone; I name you Laughter; I name you Morning Star; I name you Moon Child; I name you Deep Pool; I name you Self Healer.

> "Come forth, Woman.
> Newborn.
> New-named.
> Alive!"

When we came together again, two weeks later, P. J. Long, one of our circle of women, had taken the faith we had shared through the poems, stories, songs of our experience and had designed from those a more formal worship ritual. The rhythm of ritual moved through four phases: Self-Birthing, Group-Birthing, World-Birthing, God-Birthing.

Again, we began in darkness and silence. One woman's voice

broke the silence to tell the story of Eurynome, the Mother of all that is, the Goddess who danced the world into being and who brooded like a dove over the egg out of which came the multiplicity of creation. After the creation story, light was struck and candles were lit for the four elements: one for water, one for fire, one for earth, and one for air. The scene was set. In the mythic/sacramental time characteristic of ritual, the circle of women was transported to the Beginning and were participating in original birthing as the Original Woman.

Priscilla led us in the blessing of our bodies written by P. J.:

"Your eyes are blessed with clarity of vision. Trust what you see."

And the group responded:

"I believe in the blessing of my eyes
And in the blessing they give."

"Your ears are blessed that you may hear the voice of God within you."

"I believe in the blessing of my ears
And in the blessing they give."

"Your voice is blessed. Let it sing your truth."

"I believe in the blessing of my voice
And in the blessing it gives."

"Your hands are blessed with the magic of gentle strength."

"I believe in the blessing of my hands
And in the blessing they give."

"Your feet are blessed that you may find and walk your own true path."

"I believe in the blessing of my feet
And in the blessing they give."

"Your heart is blessed with the smile of God."

"I believe in the blessing of my heart
And in the blessing it gives."

"Your breasts are blessed with the kiss of God."

"I believe in the blessing of my breasts
And in the blessing they give."

"Your womb is blessed with all the creative energies of the Divine."

"I believe in the blessing of my womb
And in the blessing it gives."

"By the earth, who is your Great Mother,
By the water with which you were Christened,
By the fire of the Holy Spirit, in whose bosom you were created,
And by the breath of God that sustains you,
Womansoul, Womanbody, you are blessed."

After the blessing the women began to chant, combining the song with flowing hand movements that were in themselves a prayer:

"The earth, the water, the fire, the air,
Returns, returns, returns, returns . . ."

The chant became more and more quiet until only the flowing hand prayer continued in the silence. Finally, even motion stopped, and P. J. led us in a meditation of giving birth to ourselves. Centering ourselves in our birthing space, we visualized, one by one, all the colors of the rainbow and the creative power each color released within us.

We then birthed our greater selves, the group, by placing our hand on the wombs of the women sitting to each side of us in the circle, feeling the connection of our birthing energy, allowing that energy to become more and more intense until we experienced ourselves united and newborn as a circle of women. P. J. placed a handwoven blanket in the center of the circle as a symbol of the way our lives are woven together, and as we presented swatches of cloth representing our individual lives—laying those swatches on the blanket—we told stories of life's meaning for us.

Finally, Joan, a woman who had been a missionary in a third world country, told us a story representing our birthing of the world.

Gina rose and walked to the center of the circle where a chalice and two cruets of red wine were set on a small altar. She poured the wine into the chalice and presented it to us, repeating P. J.'s poems:

"Find the vision within you of what God
    is becoming through you.
And see that vision, the God of Ancient Days,
    the Birthgiver, the WomanChrist,
In this holy wine—wine that
    symbolizes the blood of renewal and of Life.

"We will pass the cup around our circle,
with each woman seeing the reflection of her
vision in the wine. We do this in silence
because, with our Jewish sisters and brothers,
we realize that the name of God, the vision we
have seen, cannot be spoken."

The cup was passed around the circle. Each woman gazed long
into the wine in silence, letting her vision, her faith, her experience of the Holy God sink into the wine. The dark surface
caught the flickering of candlelight, reflecting the union of light
and darkness where we gazed.

"Now let us share what we have seen.
Let us taste the richness of one another's vision.
Believe that in the sharing of this holy wine
that has been transformed by the vision of our
    hearts,
We not only give birth
But are birthed by one another
And by God."

Music began, softly at first and then pulsing deeper and more
loudly. A woman who had grown up in Saudi Arabia stepped
into the center of the circle. She was robed in the traditional
dress of Saudi women who are midwives to a woman in labor.
She began the birthing dance—rhythmic, throbbing. Her body
undulated with the music, first slowly, then faster and faster.
The circle swayed back and forth; we rang the traditional bells,
emphasizing the birthing beat. Her long hair flew round her
head as she twisted and bent her body. Hers was the body of
woman. Hers was our body. The dance was ours. The music
intensified. There was One Woman in the room and she was
dancing the creation dance.

At the end of the dance the dancing woman carried a basket
of red roses into the circle of women and, giving a rose to each
woman, proclaimed:

"You are a Birthgiver, clothed in the Sun."

And with that gift the worship was complete.

BIRTHING

Today's woman labors in a cosmic birthing. By the bringing forth of her self from the womb of womansoul, each woman becomes not only a metaphor but a sacrament of the birth of a transformed creation—one in which dualisms are healed and opposites reconciled.

The birth of a whole woman raises the repressed feminine from the depths, releasing her power into the world where the masculine has ruled supreme but incomplete. The birth of a whole woman gives hope for a newborn world contained in and infused with a consciousness that is embodied. This embodied consciousness, reconciling opposites and giving wholeness to the world, is what Christians call the Cosmic Christ.

Our birthing is cosmic, a Christ-birth, the revelation in creation of WomanChrist.

The worship ritual in which we engaged served to intensify and make tangible a perception I have developed from my spiritual guidance and healing work with women. Over and over, women come to me with birthing pain. Their fear of barrenness, their suspicion that they might have become barren, can be overwhelming. The desire to birth can extend from birthing a physical child to birthing a new self, a new world, or a new image of God. In listening to them and attempting to be midwife to their birthing process, I am often reminded of the prophecy of Jesus in which he compared the labor of the Christian community throughout history to the labor of a woman in childbirth. It is as if he said, "You will labor through centuries to bring forth the Christ as a woman labors to bring forth a child."

> A woman in childbirth suffers
> because her time has come;
> but when she has given birth to the child
> she forgets the suffering
> in her joy that a [person] has been born
> into the world.

So it is with you: you are sad now
but I shall see you again,
    and your hearts will be full of joy,
and that joy no one shall take from you.
                    (John 16:20–22 JB)

Is the birthing pain, now, the labor to see, in a new way, the face of the Christ?

Whether or not she has birthed an actual child, a woman understands the birthing process. Her body and psyche prepare monthly for the containment that pregnancy is, and for the release either of menstruation or, after conception and gestation, of birth. Containment and release, holding and letting go, are what women know to be the labor of creation, both physically and spiritually. It is what we do in our labor to bring forth our children, our selves, our communities, our world, our God. It is our spirituality and must be that of the Christian Church if we believe the prophecy of Jesus.

The Church has a history of calling itself "Mother"—"Mother Church." Despite the fact of its being identified through the centuries by its masculine domination, it has been "Mother." Even the men who say, "We are the Church" call themselves "Mother Church." In such ritual sacraments as baptism, the male leaders re-birth potential Church members by plunging them into the watery womb of Mother Church—the baptismal font—and bringing them forth into "new life." Many contemporary women in the Church choose not to baptize their children in protest against a practice they believe denies the holiness of woman's birthing water, which flows at the actual birth of the child. They see baptism as an effort by men to usurp womanpower by creating an image through the sacrament that it is really men who bestow life that lasts. The message that baptism speaks to these protesting women is that the life given through woman is a life toward death, whereas the life given through men in baptism is an eternal life.

Everyone, men and women alike, seems to have forgotten or cast into shadow the essentially feminine power inherent not only in baptism but in the Church as a whole. The Church is an actualization of a feminine archetype. Insofar as the Christ and the Church are one, the Christ is WomanChrist. As Church, the Christ births a new world, a cosmic new being, a transformed humankind. Baptism is a WomanChrist sacrament par excellence. In being ministers to the sacrament, men must allow themselves to live out of their anima, or feminine dimension, if they are not to be spiritually and psychologically separate from the sacramental event taking place. When women are ministers of this sacrament, they need to realize that in it the birthing power of woman is radicalized and externalized as a divine archetype in which they participate. The woman minister of baptism represents in an incarnational manner the cosmic womb of the New Creation.

Perhaps the pain associated with giving birth that women experience today heralds the rising of feminine consciousness in the world. Women experience conflict because they are expanding their consciousness of birthing power. Birthing biological children, while remaining the focus of women's experience, no longer defines the limits of that experience. In many women biological birthing becomes symbolic for birthing the self, the community, a Cosmic Consciousness, a transformed Image of God.

But we recoil in fear from that birthing. We have learned too well the "virtue" of submission. Submission—placing our woman-mission *under* or in an inferior position to the mission of men—has caused a failure of faith in our power to create. We have allowed ourselves to be subverted or, worse, have subverted ourselves, remaining undeveloped in the mistaken notion that our developmental sacrifice would benefit our children and male companions. Subversion—turning ourselves under, turning away from self—has caused a failure of will to be engaged in the creative process. By submission and subversion we deny the containment and the active letting go to birth that are the essence of our spirituality.

WOMAN AS CALDRON

Birthing dreams are common among women whose consciousness is focused on the creative process in their lives.

"I had dreamed many times that I was pregnant, but finally, in this last dream, I was actually giving birth. I was by myself in a meadow surrounded by forests. In the very center was a deep pool that reflected the sky, and when I looked into it, I

saw my face reflected as well. But my face was constantly changing, from infant to young girl to mature woman to elder-woman
and back to infant again. I watched, fascinated, as the contrac-
tions began. But unlike my actual deliveries, which were outrageously long and grueling, this one seemed pleasurable, orgasmic. I bent my body into the birthing position and in a burst
of ecstasy my girl-child was born. I washed her in the pool that
had reflected my face."

Other dreams bring out the difficulty of sustaining the new
life once born.

"I gave birth to a child and wrapped her in a white flannel
blanket. I loved her so much. But something distracted me and
I looked away. When I looked back at her, she had become so
small, no bigger than a little mouse, and her face was all wrin-
kled, as if she were an old woman. I was afraid for her, that she
would disappear entirely!"

"I have this recurring dream. I have birthed a child, and
while I am not looking it disappears. No matter how I look for
it, I can never find it again."

There are birthing dreams that are more subtle, less about
the child-self of the dreamer than about the woman as womb,
as birthgiver, as container for transformation of life.

"It is the day I am to be received into some secret society of
women. I come into a room that is entirely round, and the
women are seated in a circle around a large pot or caldron on a
tripod over a fire in the center. A priestess stirs the contents of
this caldron. One by one the initiates go to the center and gaze
into the caldron. The priestess asks them questions in a secret
language and they respond. After each woman's response, she
is given a drink of whatever is in the caldron. Finally it is my
turn. I am called to the center. The priestess looks down at me—
I am kneeling—and I am amazed to see that she is my mother.
All at once I feel a great calm, and I know I will understand the
secret language.

'Will you drink from the cup?'
'I will drink.'
'Will you be the cup?'
'I will contain the waters.'

"Then I stand to look into the caldron. Inside is a liquid rainbow transforming from color to color as the mother priestess

stirs. I am overwhelmed with a realization that I have been shown the secret of all creation, and I awake feeling totally alive."

Our birthing power consists in being a caldron, a container, in which life is transformed. Submission had become a failure of faith in ourselves as that container. Submission teaches us that we have nothing to do with the processes taking place within us, teaches that we are to be passive. But the ancient symbol of the caldron is anything but passive. In her essay "Prepatriarchal Female Goddess Images" Adrienne Rich reminds us that the first caldrons were made by women not as passive objects but as representations of the active transformative powers they felt in themselves:

It does not seem unlikely that the woman potter molded, not simply vessels, but images of herself, the vessel of life, the transformer of blood into life and milk—that in so doing she was expressing, celebrating, and giving concrete form to her experience as a creative being possessed of indispensable powers. Without her biological endowment, the child—the future and sustainer of the tribe—could not be born; without her invention and skill, the pot or vessel—the most sacred of handmade objects—would not exist.[1]

The inner space of woman is like a caldron. Her bodysoul becomes an active transformative agent just as the primitive caldron was for the tribe. The woman who crafted and used the caldron united all the worlds. She was the natural mother who bore children in the caldron of her womb and nursed them from the cup of her breast. She was the gatherer of herbs, of roots, of grains for cooking and for healing. These she stored in the caldron vessels she made from clay and grasses. In caldron pots the transformation of food took place, and in urns juice was fermented into wine.

Mother earth took the form of a caldron when caves became tombs in which burial urns were placed. Again, the womblike container held the transformative processes inherent in death and rebirth. Women served as priestesses to this cosmic process.

The ancient Chinese Book of Changes, the I Ching, also presents us with the image of the caldron. Again, the image is one of active transformation, but here it is not only transformation of the individual or the tribe but transformation on a cosmic plane. According to the I Ching, the caldron "serves in offering sacrifice to God."[2] It is the cup, or chalice, in which the ordinary is made divine. It is the image for the holy person, the prophet, or enlightened one, through whom the will of God is revealed. In the caldron earthly values are submitted to fire and, through that alchemy, become divine. So the person whom the caldron represents submits, but only to the divine fire, and sacrifices, but for the nourishment of the sacred process that creates a new world for all of humankind.

In the light of this image, women need to re-see, make re-vision in their understanding of submission. Like Mary, we sub-mit our selves only to God. "I am the handmaid of the Lord; let what you have said be done to me" (Luke 1:38 JB). We do this to fulfill our destiny of being birthgivers in the world, being birthgivers *to* the world. With other persons, whether women or men, there can be no submission. We are, instead, joined with one another in the birthing process by co-mission. We commit ourselves to the transformative birthing, and, by that commis-sion, we constellate, or bring together all the fragments of ex-perience necessary to create, the image of the caldron in our present-day world. In the power of that image and that belief about ourselves, we can preserve, nourish, and transform the world.

In this context the act of receptivity takes on new meaning. First of all, receiving *is* an *act*. Receiving is not passive. We choose to receive and to take responsibility for what we have received. We discriminate. What will we receive? When will we receive? How much will we receive? To be made to receive against our will, whether physically, psychologically, or spirit-ually, is rape; it violates us as containers of new being.

Once we have received the seed, we will give birth unless we abort that seed. If we receive the biological seed of a man, we will give birth to a child. Our power of receptivity here is enormous; we have a responsibility to choose whose seed we will preserve, nourish, and transform into a human person. Our psychological and spiritual capacity to receive also requires us to be responsible for what we take in. Once within us, it will be transformed and brought to birth. Psychological and spiritual rape violate our receptive capacity and our transformative pow-ers. Even God will not presume upon our receptivity. Mary was *asked*, not commanded, to receive the divine Seed; the responsibility she perceived combined physical, psychological, cultural, and spiritual dimensions. She was asked to be the caldron for world transformation, for incarnation of the divine. Theotokos. Mother of God. No small responsibility here. But she was not, like Leda, raped. She was asked. She could have said, "No, I cannot do that; the responsibility is beyond me." But she was not subverted by the divine Will, nor did she subvert herself. Instead she willed to con-vert—turn herself toward—the Will of God. By her active receptivity a synergy was created between her will and the divine. A power of creation was set in motion that could not have happened without her consent.

The *I Ching* shows us that the caldron needs both fire and wood—the fire of divine spirit, the wood of earth, of the human. Without the wood of Mary, there could be no Incarnation. Without her consent to receive the divine Seed, there could be no Christ. It is the intersection of will, in the free activity of human and divine, that brings about synergy—a synthesis of energy, a synthesis of will. Synergy, not subversion, is woman's secret. Her responsibility is to choose when, and under what conditions, to bring synergy about in any of the dimensions of being. Through synergy of human and divine, cosmic incarnation continues in the ongoing process of creation.

But what are the practical implications of these reflections for women in the spirituality operative in their everyday lives? Our actions, not just our images, will change. And our conversion will re-turn the image of woman in this world to its primal cluster of birthgiving and world-transforming associations. By our conversion we need to dissociate ourselves from submission and subversion. We need to contain as a caldron contains: committing ourselves to actively preserving, nourishing, transforming life in all of its dimensions. We need to release or let go of all subversion in a powerful act of will by which we intersect our will with the Will of God in a synergistic creative act.

Real women, common women, are doing this every day. Jana is one of them. During twenty years of marriage she has submitted to her husband's strong sexual needs despite her ambivalence stemming from an incest experience in her childhood. One day two months ago she said no. She claimed her right and responsibility for co-mission in order to preserve her commitment. She claimed her right and responsibility to heal her self;

to preserve, nourish, and transform her self; to give birth to herself so that she and her spouse could finally become involved in a free and synergistic co-creative act.

The women living at St. Joseph's House in Minneapolis are some of them. They have claimed their right to be. They have left marriages in which they have been battered and abused, to come to shelter, to form a caldron around one another, to be reborn in the power of their womanhood.

Annette is one of them. She had been pampered by her rich husband with beautiful things and kept by him as a lovely possession to show off to his friends. The cost to her was restriction to being simply a lovely thing. It was an easy, comfortable, submissive life. Two years ago she signed up for a class on women's issues. Her husband, confused at first by her developing womanpower, now respects her perceptions as much as he admires her beauty. She tells the group that she has been asked to assume an executive position in her husband's business. Co-mission.

Women's groups where these stories can be told become centers for developing women's spirituality. The group itself constellates the caldron for transformation and birthing. Women are discovering consciously the meaning of a process in which we have always engaged. Grouping to tell the stories of our lives is an activity that has never been absent from the community of women. We have gathered in kitchens, backyards, church basements, tea rooms, grocery stores, living rooms, by the lake, in centers for volunteerism—everywhere, anywhere—and we have told our stories. We have constellated the caldron, and we have nourished and transformed one another. Now we are beginning to realize that what we have always done is of the essence of our spiritual process.

EUCHARIST: A BIRTHING SACRAMENT

Earth is the primordial birthgiver. Earth is the caldron. Woman is earth. "Question the . . . earth," says Violaine in Paul Claudel's *Tidings Brought to Mary*, "and she will always answer you with bread and wine."[3]

When I was a young woman, a beloved teacher of mine composed a prayer that began, "O Mary, Mother of the Eucharist, prepare us for the Mass of life." I remember experiencing a conviction of my own priestliness each time I repeated the prayer. In the chapel where I prayed most often stood a tall hand-carved oak statue of Mary finished by the artist naturally in buffed wax with no paint obscuring the wood's beauty. Garbed simply in a practical but flowing work dress, Mary seemed to have been caught in the act of bringing food to her table. In one hand she held a loaf of bread, and in the other she carried a chalice of wine. Always she seemed to be offering this food to us. In my heart I called her "Mother of the Eucharist."

Priesthood is a sacramental, not physical, quality of the person. In Christian priesthood we become sacraments of Word and Eucharist. One becomes a sacrament of the Christ, and the often-repeated passage from St. Paul assures us that in Christ there is neither male nor female. In order to determine whether or not a person is "fit" for sacramental ministry, one must, it is true, take into consideration whether or not that person reflects in his or her being the outward sacramental signs. If it were true that the primary sign of Eucharist was masculine impregnating power, then, most probably, the appropriate Eucharistic priest would need to be male. But that is not what we understand by the Eucharistic sacrament.

The primary signs of Eucharistic sacrament are bread and wine—offered, transformed, shared as nourishment. The sacramental action makes present for us not only the liberating event of a multidimensional Passover (Moses and the Exodus, the death and resurrection of Jesus the Christ, the baptismal passover from the power of sin to salvation, the final passover of the Christian community into eternal communion with the Holy) but also the transformational mysteries celebrated by women since prehistory.

We have here the bread—fruit of the earth, work of human hands—baked in the oven, originally designed by women after the manner of their own bodies. We have the chalice of wine—fruit of the earth and the vine, and work of human hands—contained in the caldron of transformation, the womanwomb and womanbreast. In the sacramental action, that which has been born of earth becomes Eucharist. Thanksgiving. Earth in its most fundamental manifestations—bread, wine, woman, man—is transformed into the sacrament of the Christ.

This is a marvelous sacrament of birthing. In it woman as priest represents in her own being the container, caldron, chalice for wine that will be transformed. She is the earth in which a seed is planted and out of which grows the grain. She brings forth life. She is the oven within which grain transforms to become bread. She is apt sacrament for containment of community that, in Eucharist, experiences the alchemy of Christianing. Woman is a dimension of Eucharistic sacramentality that has been lost to the Roman Catholic tradition of Christianity. The sign cannot be complete without her.

Numerous Catholic Christian women in the Church today meet in small liturgical groups to keep alive the dimension of Eucharistic sacramentality that they, as women, embody. They celebrate Eucharist, performing acts of ecclesiastical disobedience in the service of a greater reality. They have no question but that without the actualization of the feminine dimension of the Eucharistic Mystery, that sacrament will not be whole.

Sometimes the women speak their belief in their communities: "What we are doing here *is* Eucharist." At other times, in other communities, the women celebrate with bread and wine but simply allow the signs to speak for themselves. Is it Eucharist? Each woman believes what she believes. But regardless of whether or not that belief is articulated by the community of women, the action itself has power to transform.

In living rooms, basements, attics, throughout the Christian world, women are birthing Eucharist and being birthed by it. One woman in the Wisdom House community expressed her experience as analogous to being one of the early Christians, celebrating the mysteries of birth, of death, and of resurrection in the catacombs. We are eager in our labor. We are careful in our containment and our preservation of life. We are willing in our being caldrons, vessels, chalices of transformation. Our ecclesiastical disobedience arises from our spirituality of synergy with the divine Will. We cannot acquiesce to being subverted. It arises from our spirituality of co-mission, which submits to no one but God. Such is our responsibility as containers of new life. Such is our right as birthgivers.

In December the Wisdom House community gathered around an elaborately braided loaf of Christmas bread. In our hope for the world and in solidarity with all the life the earth brings forth, we dressed the bread with fruits and nuts of our earth. We prayed with each additional decoration for the transformation of our world in peace and justice, patience, joy, and nurturing love. Then the community of women extended hands over the bread and let the blessing of the Holy One transform all—the women and bread contained in the center of the womancircle. We broke the bread then and gave it to one another, saying: "Take and eat. This is the bread of the Christ Mass."

Eucharist? I believe so. Cosmic birthing? Absolutely! Earth we have always been. We are Eucharist. We are birthing WomanChrist.

Part Two

WOMANPOWER, WOMANWISDOM

CHAPTER 9

Releasing the Victim

"Man is the priest," says Paul Claudel, "but it is not forbidden to woman to be victim."[1] The image calls forth the worst in sadomasochistic inflation: woman on the cross, sacrificing herself for the world, at the judgment and in the power of the male priest. In this image both women and theology are abused. And yet most women would recognize their reality in it, and many would admit to believing in a victimizing theology.

In the attempt to be acceptable to God, numerous women throughout the Christian era have submitted themselves to the worst abuse out of faith in the words of St. Paul: "Wives should be submissive to their husbands as if to the Lord because the husband is head of his wife just as Christ is head of his body the church, as well as its savior. As the church submits to Christ, so wives should submit to their husbands in everything" (Eph. 5:22–24 NAB). Fathers, too, have traditionally held spiritual power over their daughters. In the laws of the Church that were still operative in modern times, fathers possess the power to cancel vows their daughters have made to God. The Church seems to assume God would "take the man's point of view" on the matter.

We have many stories of young women fighting marriages imposed on them by fathers who "canceled" their vows of virginity. St. Clare, St. Catherine of Siena, and St. Elizabeth of Hungary are only a few. Ironically, the Church later recognized the sanctity of these women, which consisted in no small part of their refusal to obey their fathers. Submission to anything less than God victimizes the soul. It destroys life and creative energy. It sets one wandering in a wilderness where chaos reigns.

Each week I see women who identify themselves as victims: victims of sexual abuse, incest, marital violence; of patriarchal power in business, government, and church; of abandonment and neglect. The list goes on. They feel lost, powerless, shameful, confused, despairing, and doomed to continue submitting themselves to further victimization. Some have become angry; that's good, for anger in a victim is the beginning of hope and the restoration of justice.

You know the stories.

Martha's family was large, and she was among the youngest. Her mother and father had little time to spend with her, so she needed to be satisfied with what parental affection and care she could get from her older siblings. At fourteen she felt lonely, hopeful about love, uncertain about herself. Her drama teacher paid special attention to her, singled her out for a lead role in the freshman play, requested her help in the school theater after classes. It was not long before he "ravished" her, initiating her into erotic secrets through sexual "play." She loved him. How could she help it? He was gentle; he had chosen her; he was a king, a father-lover, she a princess. But she was only fourteen years old. He was thirty and married.

The priest in the confessional told her she was sinning because she was making love with a man who was already married. She must, therefore, take the responsibility for stopping her violation of the holy sacrament of matrimony. But the drama teacher's seductive power won out over the condemnations of the priest. In a combination of terrifying guilt and compelling pleasure she was caught as in a trap.

After her freshman year, the drama teacher simply abandoned her, going to another town to teach, without saying goodbye.

Now, at thirty years of age, she wants relief from shame, from an emptiness within, from inability to find pleasure in her spouse, from a sense of overwhelming meaninglessness. But she feels that there is nothing she can do to reclaim her lost self. She says she is a victim of powerlessness.

Lisa began her career in the church enthusiastically. (Enthusiasm is the energy from the gods.) Convinced that she was gifted by God to nurture the soul of humankind, she set out to educate herself. She achieved degrees in theology. She developed skill in communication. She learned the art of spiritual healing. She gave herself to a life of prayer. Then she sought a ministry in a hospital because she wanted most to be with people who were crying out from the pain in their lives. But hospitals were not hiring "nonsacramental" ministers. Being Roman Catholic, she could not be ordained to priesthood and therefore could not become a sacramental minister. She tried religious education. It was not her calling. She worked for women's ordination. She worked for ten years and then the Pope issued a statement that women could not be ordained because they did not "resemble Jesus." Finally she gave up. Her life feels dry and listless. She says that everything is dust. She wonders if she believes in God anymore. She says she is a victim of the patriarchy.

Allison loves a priest. He is pastor of her parish, and she had always been active in parish committees. She had never before met a man who truly understood her and with whom she could share her developing spirituality. The relationship deepened in intensity. He spent considerable time at her apartment; they talked until late hours; one night they were unable or unwilling to keep the spiritual dimension of their relationship disconnected from the wholeness of themselves, and they made love. After that, she felt he would eventually leave the active priesthood and marry her, even though he explained again and again that priesthood was the essence of his life and that without it he would be no one.

She thought of breaking off the relationship, painful as that would be for her. She tried. But he called; he showed up at her apartment; he pleaded with her. It seemed that she had also become part of the essence of his life. He wanted both Allison and his priesthood. He asked her to keep the secret of their love. He asked her to keep herself available for him alone. He told her that it was a spiritual thing, that it was *their* priesthood. What he had learned about life through her he could now use in helping others. She would be his hidden, but powerful, soul. She tried. Soon the secrecy of her life began consuming her. Looking at him, she realized that he had everything he wanted: his priesthood, a public self, a private life with her. She felt responsible for protecting him, keeping their love a secret. She could not appear in public as his companion. She had to learn cool detachment toward him at meetings, pretending to be simply another of his congregation. She felt herself begin to die a bit inside. She says she is a victim of the "system's" celibacy laws.

No doubt each woman reading this chapter has a story of victimization to tell—probably more than one. She has, perhaps, heard so many stories from friends that her head reels from the pain of them. She is tired from containing the exhaustion that being a victim seems to cause. She is tired of the exhaustion of her friends. She feels abandoned by something essential to her life, and she is not sure she remembers what it is.

There are probably as many ways of victimizing a person as there are people to victimize. The point is, most victims can point to some traumatic experience endured at a specific time in their lives, or over a long period of time. That experience provoked a response of retreat—of something vital to themselves retreating and finally being lost. Without that "something" the person cannot live in desire and in hope, cannot produce creatively, cannot feel that life is worthwhile. I suggest that that "something" is eros.

In our culture we have limited eros to sex, and by so doing we have literalized it and pushed underground its vital spiritual power. This is a dangerous situation for us, since any numinous power—such as eros—that is denied, rejected, repressed becomes daimonic in its entrapment. It smolders in our depths and will eventually break forth either destructively or creatively, and probably both. Nothing, no energy that is within us, actively seeks to destroy us. But if we have denied any energy long enough, it seeks so powerfully to be incorporated into the self that it can explode, and in so doing can explode the soul, or psyche, along with it. In the desolation that follows, in the exhaustion of this essential psychic energy, we experience what is called psychosis. Then, rather than the creative wholeness we could have enjoyed by incorporation of psychic energy, we experience psychic fragmentation and chaos. Our souls are lost and set to wander the wastelands of life in search of a lost god.

Eros is a god. He is passion, the vital energy to create, to reach toward what might be and actualize it. In Greek mythology he is the original creator; his arrows pierce the earth, which then springs forth, green. Eros is yearning. He is desire. Paul Tillich associates eros with our passion for meaning and value. And St. Augustine identifies eros as the power that impels us toward

God. The loss of eros, and one's resignation to that loss, leaves a person passionless, sterile, without vision of possibilities, empty of meaning and value for life, and with a conviction of powerlessness to change one's situation. Stuck in our powerlessness, believing there is nothing we can do to remedy the barrenness of our situation (the god attends us only at his own free will), we are victims. If we remain in that state, Psyche, the soul, will die.

How does the loss of eros happen? Practically speaking—that is, in the context of our daily human lives—it usually happens as a result of a real victimization. A trusted father appears one night in the bedroom of his little girl and rapes her. The physical wound heals, but the soul loses something essential, withers, and becomes dry.

VICTIMIZATION AND CHRISTIANITY

The Christian woman can find herself caught in the deepest and most destructive of victimizations, one that drives a wedge into womansoul, sundering an essential wholeness. She is warned that she is, by nature, Eve—that by being a woman she inherits insidious power allied with the evil one, which, if not subdued by submission and obedience to her father or husband, could contaminate and finally destroy humanity. However, if she renounces her fundamental Eve-like nature and embraces a life either of obedient virginity or of submissive motherhood, she can save not only herself but also the fathers, husbands, and sons she serves. She becomes like Mary, immaculately conceived and safely sexless.

This Eve/Mary split applied to daily interactions between men and women becomes the source of and the justification for any victimization we can imagine. In the woman herself, the split ensures the loss of eros. Any hope or desire dries up in the desert of her despoiled womansoul. She can only wander, powerless. Her "Eve nature" justifies punishment, she is told. She can be raped, battered, dominated, exiled. When she is seen as "Mary," she is honored but patronized, protected but excluded from decision making, seen as pure but without passion. Again, eros is lost.

She also loses womansoul.

Before being in the image of either Eve or Mary, womansoul is in the image of Psyche. It is our return to Psyche as WomanChrist that can heal the victimizing dualism that has become a part of Christian imagery over the centuries.

THE IMAGE OF PSYCHE

Of all that is not God, Psyche is most beautiful—youngest daughter of the Creator, delicate as dawn, powerful as spring. Her eyes pool the original deeps; her heart pulses with the yearning of the whole world. She appears in our dreams, a woman coming forth from the chrysalis of unconsciousness to rise on wings—a butterfly.

Psyche is essence of earth, translucence of matter, container of mysteries. Out of her flows all desire, all intensity, all feeling. It is she who moves us to unite with our loves and to mourn whatever dies. She is passion and innocence, sensation and insight, opacity and brilliance. Her beauty seduces by its nature, and those who give up control by responding to her lure find beauty everywhere.

She is the mother of pleasure and bliss. Without her gift, ecstasy must remain forever absent from life.

Psyche searches always for her God. Outrageously, she defies convention, undertakes any task, endures any danger, including death, to find him. Humbly, she bows down before the divine Will. She becomes the servant of all creation and is crowned with stars.

Psyche reflects the original union of creation, containing all possibilities. She is light and shadow, power and fragility, mind and body, simplicity and complexity, life and death. The fundamental paradox of her nature influences her every choice, through which the process of creation continues.

Psyche is Soul—womansoul. In her, Eve and Mary are, and have always been, one.

ORIGINAL SIN

In both the creation myth of Judeo-Christian tradition and the Greek myth of Eros and Psyche, womansoul is driven from the garden of original union as the result of betrayal. Both Eve and Psyche lose confidence in themselves and submit to what is less than God. That submission splits womansoul. The chasm opens to the center of life, from which Eros—the power of and desire for life—escapes. Eve (woman) and Psyche (soul) then begin the journey of humankind: to recover Eros by healing the sundered self.

In Christianity we name this sundered condition Original Sin. The horror of Christian history is that we have made and continue to make real women the scapegoats for humanity's sundered soul and the resulting loss of eros. By setting up an Eve/ Mary dichotomy, we perpetuate the split. We assure an everlasting victim. We institutionalize dualism, which is the essence of Original Sin. Consequently, we trivialize eros, separate sexuality from both love and the full expression of life, and inhibit the creative process.

Accepting a dualistic image of ourselves, we become wanderers with wounded and lost souls—victims and victimizers.

MARY

If making Mary and Eve opposites perpetuates a condition of Original Sin and keeps real women in a state of victimization, how can Christian women claim Mary or Eve as an image of woman? We cannot. We need to look more deeply at both Mary and Eve, seeing them with the new vision of womansoul.

Mary images Psyche as WomanChrist. She reconciles the opposites by refusing to submit to what is less than God. She is Eve (woman) and Psyche (soul) healed and whole because of her total response to what is only God. In her image we conquer dualism and release the victim within us.

A part of the Mary myth is that she was conceived and born without Original Sin. She is by nature the *whole* woman. She is the new Eve—the woman who contains within herself all the opposites: light and shadow, fragility and power, creation and destruction, submission and refusal—and she has confidence in her essential goodness. She is not split. Eros, the power of life, dwells in her.

"Hail Mary, full of grace," heralds the angel of the annunciation. "God is with you!" Mary *full* of blessing, original gift, cosmic integrity. Mary not opposite of Eve, but rather the wholeness of Eve. Mary is Eve refusing victimization. Every woman stands in the image of Mary when, despite any violence of body or soul done to her, she holds to the belief in her power of love. Through her, not only life but the Christ is born into the world.

CONSEQUENCES OF VICTIMIZING DUALISM

Belief in womansoul's power of life requires great courage, for the violence perpetrated on us has been and continues to be massive. Each of us feels not only the violence making victims of us personally but also each wound inflicted on any woman. Each of us is raped at gunpoint and killed alongside a Salvadoran road with Sr. Ita Ford, Sr. Maura Clarke, Sr. Dorothy Kazel, and Jean Donovan. Each feels the threat of exclusion from profession, Church, or religious order for speaking and acting with conscience. We are taken from our children and locked in prison for being promoters of peace. Every joke meant to trivialize women diminishes us all. When one of us is patronized, made a "token," all of us are weakened.

If we blame men alone for our victimization, we lack justice and perpetuate another form of the very dualism that made us victims in the first place. Women also victimize themselves and each other. All of us, men and women, seem victims of a pervasive unconsciousness. In it the creative feminine is imprisoned and devalued, driven from the paradise of the soul. Such devaluing continues the sin of dualism. Women or men who devalue the feminine within themselves can become violent toward her, either in themselves or in other persons.

Women who have been victims of incest as children, for example, often find their rage directed toward themselves and other "victims."

Gloria hated herself and had attempted suicide three times. When she came to see me, she made her position clear from the beginning.

"I am a victim. Incest. My Goddamn father. I've seen scores of therapists and I'm done with that. Maybe something spiritual will help. If you don't feel comfortable with all of this, tell me now. Don't waste my time pretending. I hate weak women."

The truth was, I didn't feel comfortable; I felt attacked by the victim in her. I felt her trying to ferret out the victim in me, to see how weak I might be, maybe to do violence to that fragile, wounded part of my own soul. I felt in her an intense hatred for anything that could be victimized, including herself, including me.

RELEASING THE VICTIM: A PROCESS

Before we can be free of victimization, we need to engage in a process of releasing the victim. As with any process, it is composed of stages:

1. Recognizing the victimization
2. Accepting the victim
3. Confronting the victimizer
4. Releasing the victim

RECOGNIZING THE VICTIMIZATION

Perhaps the most wrenching hurt comes from first seeing the victim within us—however she came to be there. We avoid her as we are tempted to avoid anyone in extreme and inconsolable pain. I remember working with a beautiful, sensitive woman who had experienced sexual abuse from her mother when she was a child. She spoke aloud of the images that appeared to her in a waking dream during our session together. All at once she gasped. Crouched in a corner of her soul hid a dirty, frightened, injured little girl. The child reminded her of nothing more than a trapped, wild animal, dangerous because of its outrage and outrageous condition, but pitiable as well.

The woman began to weep and, through her tears and sobs, to cry out, "Oh, no! No! Oh, the poor little thing! Oh, *no! Oh!* I know her—I *know her!*"

She had seen and recognized the victim within her.

Such recognition does not always elicit pity. Anger and self-hatred can and often do accompany the awareness in us that we have taken so much abuse—absorbed so much violence—that we actually contain, actually *are*, a victim. Some people fight so hard to deny the victim within, at the same time hating that victim with such intensity, that they become violent toward others whom they perceive as victims. They project the victim that is a part of themselves onto someone else and seek to destroy her there. The victim thus becomes a victimizer.

Only when each of us recognizes the victim within will this violent cycle stop.

ACCEPTING THE VICTIM

Our first inclination upon recognizing the victim in ourselves is to punish her, to act toward her as the victimizer always did, with violence.

"You are ugly and hateful and do nothing right! It is because of you that my life is a mess. You are puny, weak, and a coward. It's no wonder no one loves me; no matter how hard I try to hide you, you always come out. And who could love you? I hate you. I wish you were dead!" It is not uncommon for a woman to attempt to kill the victim through suicide. Even those of us who do not engage in such extremes of destruction can make ourselves quite miserable with the self-denial that comes of punishing the victim within.

Many women have found it helpful to begin regarding the victim within them as a wounded child. This transformation of attitude toward that facet of themselves can take much time and patience. It isn't so easy as sometimes presented in popular literature, which would lead us to think that all we need do is take the wounded child in our arms, hold her, tell her she is loved, "parent" her in a healing fashion, and she will cause us no more trouble. No. This child is wild, angry, and often hateful. She has been taught so well and often that she is worthless that she believes it. We are not only re-parenting the wounded child within; we are taming the wild one.

One client of mine who had understood for years the dynamics of healing the wounded child, and who has patiently and consistently practiced this loving discipline toward that facet of her self, still experiences the violence of her early victimization. She writes:

"Even though I understand the reasons for what is happening to me, I can't get rid of the shame. At the most inopportune moments shame clouds my soul so darkly that it takes all my energy and belief to give any love to myself at all. I feel so hopeless then. So . . . bad. If I can be quiet and repeat a sort of mantra—'Peace, little child, you are loved'—then I can be freed at least from violence. Not from pain.

"When will I ever be finished with this struggle?"

I suspect that the process of releasing the victim, and each phase of that process, continues throughout our lives in ever-widening spirals. Perhaps in our times, when the repressed and victimized feminine is rising to become powerful again, no woman is free of this process. It is our destiny. It is our contribution to the healing of the world.

CONFRONTING THE VICTIMIZER

A time always comes in the healing process for the victim to confront the victimizer. It is a time for telling the truth, for unveiling the shame as a lie.

Confrontation has its proper time. If a person confronts the victimizer before she has accepted the victim within herself, then she risks repeating the victimization. Either she will allow the victimizer to revictimize her or she will become the victimizer herself and retaliate. Then confrontation becomes vengeance.

Confrontation needs to be for healing, for repairing the split, for weaving back together what is torn. We confront. We stand facing one another. We reveal who we are because of one another. Dualism is overcome. By accepting the victim within myself, I am freed of any need to victimize another. Then I can stand face to face with the actual person or group or institution that has victimized me. I can recognize the dualistic split that causes the victimizer. And I can tell the truth about the violence perpetrated by that split. I can tell the truth about the wounding of my own soul and the victimizer's responsibility in that wounding. I can face the one who did violence to me, knowing that he no longer has power to hurt me.

But it is not sufficient to confront the person or persons outside of me who have done violence to womansoul. I must also confront the victimizer within myself. When we are victimized, we learn to victimize ourselves and others. I must also tell the truth to that victimizer within.

The confrontation needs to transcend rage. We feel enraged when we recognize the victim within, and outraged when we remember the violence we took into ourselves. But the rage dissipates when we accept the victim. By the time we are ready to confront the victimizer, we may feel anger and sorrow as they are connected to the truth of what happened in the victimization. But rage, which can only continue the cycle of violence, needs to be gone.

RELEASING THE VICTIM

Meg, a friend of mine, recently talked with me about a mutual acquaintance who has been in incest therapy for seven years. "I am really concerned," Meg mused, "because she seems to have lost everything in herself except her identity as a victim. It is all she talks about. She explains everything about her life with her 'victimhood.' It is almost as if being a victim is her new reason for being. It has become like a cause. 'I am a victim. That is who I am. That is all I am. That is what gives my life meaning.' To tell you the truth, I feel we are losing *her*. There was a beautiful, complex person there once; now all I can see is a victim."

Eventually, we need to release the victim. As with each other phase of the process, we will be releasing her again and again as we spiral into deeper and deeper awarenesses of the violence done to the feminine within us. But to hold onto that facet of ourselves, to keep cuddling the wounded child, retards and finally stops our growth as individuals and, ultimately, as a society.

Releasing the victim requires strength of soul, the tenaciousness of Psyche accomplishing the tasks given her by Aphrodite, goddess of love, as a prerequisite to recovering Eros. Only when the victim is released will Eros wing his way back into our souls.

PSYCHE'S TASKS

When Psyche loses Eros, she wanders a desolate wilderness. Her passion for life, her sense of self, courage, and beauty die. Womansoul victimized becomes wilderness—original chaos. From that inner whirling can come either a new creation or an everlasting wasteland. The outcome depends on becoming free of identification with the chaos, that sundering that tears apart the fundamental unity of creation.

Before Psyche can release the victim within her, she must accomplish four difficult and complex tasks. Regarded psychologically, these tasks are the work of inter- and intrapsychic restructuring. Regarded spiritually, these tasks are the work by which womansoul transforms through faith to become WomanChrist.

The myth speaks in metaphor. Psyche (soul) wanders the wilderness (chaos, nothingness). She must become participant in forming wilderness into a new creation. How? Sort grain. Gather golden fleece. Contain water in crystal. Descend to the underworld to bring back the beauty of Persephone.

SORT GRAIN

In the soul of a victim, confusion reigns, like quantities of wheat, barley, millet, lentils, beans, poppy seed, and vetch spilled together on the granary floor. "I'm all mixed up. Are these my feelings or yours, my responsibilities or someone else's? When I want to scream, rage, cry, run away for the pain of it, who is it screaming? Who is running? Is it I? Is it some ancient child who remembers violence that no longer appears clear to me? Or is the crying that of the Stranger of God, caught in the dark bowels of the world and weeping with the tears of all women? What is 'in' and what is 'out'? What is mine or yours or everyone's? How can I sort this out?"

The task: differentiation. The wheat in one pile, then the barley, the millet, the lentils, and so on until each element is identified and put in order. But the process, surprisingly, is not one of taking control. Power fails to be helpful here.

When chaos overwhelms us, the soul knows itself to be powerless to organize reality by the normal means of reason and choice. Rather than taking charge, one must take time, and wait. Rather than thought, contemplation comes to our aid. The sorting happens at an almost primitive depth, where instinct reigns, deeper than the the betraying lies that prompted the original victimization and consequent chaos. Like one practicing Zen, womansoul must sit still as the feelings, memories, voices, images pass through her. No matter the turbulence they seek to cause, she must sit still while they find their proper place in her life. And as she is still and as she waits, she experiences that the violence has not destroyed her, nor have the seductions enticed her to become what she is not.

Things fall into place. The grain is sorted. The victim can begin to be released.

GATHER GOLDEN FLEECE

We continue to live in a world where violence threatens and where, if we intend to live fully, we must encounter aggression. The most beautiful of all wool, golden fleece, grows only on dangerously aggressive rams who would kill Psyche were she to attempt to take it from them directly. Instead, she must wait until the serene waters of the river lull the rams to sleep. Then she can enter the grove and gather the fleece from every thorn and briar to which it has attached itself.

When we place ourselves in victimizing situations, we risk the death of womansoul. Confronting the enraged ram—the *aggression* of the victimizer—will not make us strong but will destroy us. Such confrontation simply repeats the original victimization. Nevertheless, we need something from the aggressor. There is a kind of life energy of which the aggression is the shadow side. The soul must re-store this energy in order to be re-formed. The golden fleece has the same meaning as the Kingdom of Heaven, the Pearl of Great Price, or the Holy Grail. It is a symbol of transformation of the profane into the sacred. In alchemy it is akin to the philosopher's stone, which metaphorically, was believed to change lead into gold.

But we are forbidden to take this transforming agent aggressively, for by so doing we would release its shadow side. Aggression releases aggression. Rather, transformation must be received as a gift, respected and collected.

CONTAIN WATER IN CRYSTAL

Psyche stands on the mountain with a crystal jar given her by the goddess of love. The mountainside drops precipitously to the torrential river Styx, which gushes forth from the center of the slippery rock. The sacred water of life is guarded by snakelike dragons. Somehow Psyche must fill the crystal jar with the sacred water and return it safely to Aphrodite. The task looms hopelessly impossible. The waters sing out to her.

"Be off! Be off! What do you wish, wish, wish? Look! Look! Where are you at, are you at? Care, take care! Off with you, off with you, off with you! Death! Death!"[2]

We need to learn our limits. The only way to collect the water is not to collect it. To fill the crystal jar we must give the jar away.

Fragile as crystal, the victimized feminine must be filled with the sacred and returned to love. The task is a spiritual one. Here on the boundaries between this world and another, womansoul learns that she is not God and cannot accomplish the tasks proper to the Divine. Not by her own work will womansoul become WomanChrist. She cannot fill the fragile crystal with the sacred water of Life. "What do you wish, wish, wish?" Each must answer the question, and, in the process, "Care, take care!"

The task is faith. Although womansoul must contain water in crystal if the victim is to be released and Eros regained, she cannot make this containment happen. The limits are clear. Containing the sacred water of Life in the crystal soul is a task beyond our power.

Psyche stands on the precipice, holds the crystal jar, and waits with care. And the Divine Eagle, seeing her faith and taking compassion on her, soars to the mountaintop, grasps the crystal jar in his beak, and descends to where the water gushes from the rock. There he fills the crystal and returns it to Psyche's keeping.

DESCEND TO THE UNDERWORLD

One more task remains. To release the inner victim and recover Eros, the woman must journey to the place within herself that she experiences as dead. Here the source of her victim identification is located. This is the throne of Persephone, the goddess of springtime, who was raped and stolen by Hades, god of the underworld. She is the mythic victim infused with omnipotence. And she reigns in every victimized woman. Psyche's task is to bring the beauty of Persephone back to the surface.

Deep in the unconscious, a distillation process produces beauty from the energy released in a victim's struggle to survive. This is a beauty so profound that it is rarely claimed. The woman aware of its presence in her has stood face to face with her own death. Consciousness of Persephone's beauty costs transcendence of death. The way is descent to the underworld of womansoul. Not only does the inner victim need recognition and acceptance; she also needs consciousness of her beauty distilled from survival and transformation.

Beauty risen from the underworld of womansoul glows through a woman as wisdom and power. She attracts Eros with

such beauty, and in their reunion creative energy releases pleasure. Everything she undertakes, then, seems to originate in wisdom and proceed with the power of creation. When the beauty
rises to the surface and the woman lives from it, womansoul
becomes WomanChrist.

WOMANCHRIST IN THE CHURCH

Droves of women are leaving the Church. They are refusing
to be victims to a system that has abused them for centuries.
They are leaving, often silently, after enduring unbelievable
pain. Their absence is hardly noticed by the leaders, since their
presence was hardly noticed previously.

They are women like Donna, a professional nurse, and a
mother of three adolescent children, who simply began staying
home on Sunday when the family went to mass. After having
not seen her for over a year, I ran into her at a large funeral of
a well-known local doctor. She was standing in the vestibule
weeping. I went up to her, put my arm around her, and asked
if she had been close to the deceased. "No," she whispered.
"No, I was close to the Church. This is the first time I've been
back for over a year, and it reminded me of all the beauty I have
had to give up." I inquired about her reasons for absenting herself from something she obviously loved so much, and she responded: "I couldn't bear the constant exclusion in words and
actions from a Mystery that is so essential to me. I can be more
faithful to God if I stay away from the Church."

Often a woman who has left the Church simply develops her
own spirituality and lives it alone. But most women need some
kind of community. Many try Wicca communities—covens of
women who ritualize the mysteries of the universe in ways that
radically express nature and the feminine.

For some, Wicca provides an answer. For others, the commitment to Jesus Christ and the Christian Mystery remains essential and Wicca seems too partial. So they seek to create communities of their own. In these communities women's mysteries
and experiences are explored, validated, and celebrated and connections are sought with each woman's Christian faith. The Wisdom House Worship Community referred to in chapter 8 is one
of these groups. I have often heard the women express the con-

viction that what we are doing is analogous to the worship experiences of the early Christians in the catacombs. "We are engaged in a transformative process here, a renewal of the Christian Church."

If women are to remain within the Church and not be victims, we must be willing to engage in the tasks of Psyche in relationship to that institution. We must sort out the immense confusion. We must gather the golden fleece (the Pearl of Great Price, the Kingdom of Heaven) from those who hold all the power. We must collect water from the river of Life in the crystal chalice of our spirit. And, finally, we must be willing to descend to the depths and to bring the wise and powerful beauty of Persephone back to the surface of the world. In other words, we must take responsibility for the unique gift of ourselves and not dissolve into the collective by sacrificing ourselves for the continuation of an abusive system. We must become ourselves and commit our love and courage, our power and feeling, to renewal and the ongoing creation of the Christian community.

We will be feared. We will be ridiculed sometimes. Occasionally, we will be "excommunicated." We will often be ignored and our presence and work denied. It will feel like wandering in the wilderness. Whether we remain within the institution of the Church or find we can only keep our faith in God by crossing its boundaries and entering the lonely places outside, we will be in diaspora. We have always been in diaspora within the Church because the wholeness of who we are as women has been rejected—because we have never been allowed full participation.

Only a commitment to erotic justice can redeem the Christian community and heal the division that has been so abusive to women. This kind of justice requires a love that includes but transcends those loves represented by Eros, Aphrodite, and Persephone. This is a love that brings a person to full actualization—to wholeness—and at the same time inspires the gift of everything to God. This is the kind of gift that integrates, that lets loose the creative spirit of God in the world. The response in love not hindered by the monstrous forces of disintegration is always a gift—grace. It is in those times and situations when we perceive love to be an impossibility—a response beyond our strength—and yet *do* love, that we are most aware of this love as a gift. The gift, the grace, of love is not separate from our own capacity to love. Rather, the gift empowers all the love within us and transforms it. It is simple, for that which is integrated has transcended complexity. The gift of God is most intense in our experience of our humanness, whole and free to respond.

Such love is not without pain. The love of Jesus that resulted in crucifixion was such a love. Jesus transcended victimhood by confronting victimization but not acquiescing to it. He died but only seemed to be conquered. He never lost his integrity; he never submitted to what was less than God. He held to his vision both of himself and of God. The ancient Easter sequence states the mystery of it:

> "Together, death and life
> In a strange conflict strove,
> The Prince of life, who died,
> Now lives and reigns."

He overcame the dualism that threatened to make victims of us all. The crucifixion contains a wonderful paradox for those who can see through the surface to the meaning of this event. The one who seems to be the victim—Jesus—is not the victim at all. In him we see the way in which we victimize ourselves. He is who we are at best. He is what we kill in being less than we can be. But he lives and reigns. Those who do the killing are the victims of this event.

Diaspora contains the same paradox. The Mystery of God's Love finds its most radical expression in the death and resurrection of Jesus the Christ. Crucifixion is, finally, the gift expressed in the life of every person who bears his name and gives over the very great capacities of humanness to a readiness to be love. Such love undertakes a descent into the depths believing in the rising of a greater life—a more beautiful love. Such love is the intense search for one's true identity, one's most essential name. In this love Eros is transformed into the urging (*Charitas Christi urget nos*) that makes of us an eschatological people, yearning for the fulfillment of the whole People of God, the New Heaven and the New Earth. Through transformed Eros we redeem the time and the dream, both living in the center in the present and creating the future at whose edge we are poised. Such love, transformed, is no easy relationship between persons—no simple mutual love providing one another with comfort. It is, rather, a divine love infused with characteristic *tremens et fascinens*. This love reaches deep to what is most real, and the person who experiences it can be willing to sacrifice everything to free it into the world.

The experience of diaspora challenges all love. Diaspora dis-illusions. But true self is gained through the sacrifice of illusion— a dis-illusioned self. Diaspora throws one into chaos. But love embraces the wilderness experience that the community is unable to embrace and, by so doing, re-visions the radical ideal of the community. Diaspora is a rejection experience. But love seeks mutuality with those who reject by taking on the tasks of Psyche and strengthening one's soul. Diaspora differentiates a person from the loved community. But love urges us to stand apart in order to call the community to a recognition of its deepest reality. We enter the essential reality of the community by love's self-imposed exile.

The love of women in diaspora struggles against separation and alienation toward unity. But not an easy unity. Our very existence in diaspora places a judgment on the Christian institutions. At the same time, our exile calls the Christian community to repentance. From our place in exile it is as if we are calling out: "I judged you unjust and you cast me out. In many ways I stand apart from you, but I will not let you go. It is from you I have come, and though you now refuse to recognize me as your offspring, I claim you. I will not let you go, and if necessary I will drag you with me, kicking and screaming, into the future. I will not let you go (as Jacob said to his daimon, who was also his God) until you bless me."

This love that releases the victim in us, frees us to be, and opens the passageways for creation is a love that rends the soul. It is powerful in a Tillichian sense: it maintains its being, open to the forces that seek to destroy it with nonbeing more powerful than hatred—simple indifference. It is a love that is faithful to promise. In the midst of those who would say, "You are no longer who you are. You have forfeited your name, Christian, by being a woman in diaspora," this love says, "I *am*, for I have become *WomanChrist*."

CHAPTER 10

Welcoming the Many

Some years ago, after reading some of the works of Carl Gustav Jung and intuiting in his thought and experience a strong affinity with my own, I sought out a Jungian analyst, hoping to acquire from her both a deeper appreciation of Jungian thought and an integration of what felt like disparate energies within myself. For days before my first meeting with her my excitement grew. At night I dreamed that she was a guru in a schoolhouse with a library stacked with ancient bottles full of alchemical potions.

I walked up to Lyn Cowan's house early in the morning on a crisp October day. Everything in nature seemed gold and blue. Leaves drifted lazily from the trees, covering what green grass still remained. The sky, through the almost bare branches of elm trees, appeared more blue than at any other time of the year, contrasted as it was with the leaves' gold. Eagerly and a little nervously, I knocked on her door.

Two kittens, Dunkin and Willie, skittled up and tumbled in play at my feet when I stepped into Lyn's tiny living room–office. "You don't mind cats, do you?" she grinned. She was a little nervous, too, I thought, and I relaxed a bit. After I assured her that cats and I got along just fine, she offered me a cup of coffee, motioned for me to sit in one of two identical easy chairs, and asked me what it was that brought me to her.

"I want to get myself together," I began. "There seems to be a lot of conflict in my life, especially at work, and I want to be integrated so that I can deal with it."

She laughed. "You would probably do better if you could come apart."

During the years since then, I have often had occasion to be reminded of that outrageous burst of wisdom. At the time I had no idea what Lyn meant; I almost didn't hear her, the notion felt so foreign to what I thought I was doing there. It was because I felt "apart" that I had gone to her; what possible benefit could there be in "coming apart"? Wasn't that what happened to people when they became emotionally and psychologically ill? They collapsed. They disintegrated. They came apart. I let the comment go, slipping by it into a further explanation of who I was and what I wanted from her. Only many months later, after I had untangled the web of the many persons within me, did she remind me of my initial goal. Then we both laughed.

Those who continue to remind me are women who come to me for spiritual guidance. A sense of disintegration accompanied by the "loss of God" often motivates women to seek a spiritual guide. "My life is falling apart," they mourn. "Tell me what to do to put myself back together." It isn't surprising that we would conclude that putting ourselves back together would be the answer to our pain. "Wholeness is holiness" has become the byword of much spirituality. We are strongly influenced by the notion. Besides that, it is probably true. An ancient belief of most of the world's great spiritual traditions is that God is One and human beings' fullness is to be whole and one with God. When we are whole, the contradictions of our nature will be resolved and we will live in simplicity.

When I asked my Jungian analyst to help me get myself together, I had forgotten—or had never understood in the first place—the wry reprimand of Mother Ann. She was novice director of the convent where I spent my youth. I was eighteen years of age and just beginning to realize the complexities and contradictory energies I contained. The complaint of St. Paul became mine: "That which I would do, I don't; and that which I would not do, I find myself doing. Oh, wretched being that I am!" Surely one of the most universally human laments in the Christian scriptures.

In the convent in those days, before the Second Vatican Council, we had a practice of kneeling beside each sister and asking for her prayers. Being so aware of my complexity and the trouble it always caused me, and also having read of the wholeness, purity of intention, singleness of vision, and simplicity of the "saints," I lit upon simplicity as the answer to my problem. So I asked for the sisters' prayers. With my veil lowered over my face and my hands hidden in my long sleeves, I moved one evening from sister to sister in the convent dining room murmuring "Sister, I humbly ask you to pray that God might grant me the gift of simplicity." In accord with tradition, the sisters kept silence and did not look at me as I made my plea. But prayers were assured, and I felt wonderfully relieved and as though the resolution of my problems lay just a moment into the future.

Immediately after dinner, Mother Ann called me into her office.

"Don't you *ever* do that again, Sister!"

"Do what, Mother?" I asked, confused.

"Don't you ever ask for *simplicity!* God alone is simple. Who do you think you are? Simplicity, my stars! You foolish girl! My word—simplicity, is it?! By the time you are holy enough to ask for simplicity, you will be too humble to ask. I have never heard of anything so grandiose! Eighteen years old and wanting *simplicity!* My dear sister, my foolish child, pray for possible things. Pray to be kind. Pray to be less vain. Pray to notice the needs of others. Don't ever again pray for simplicity!"

I forgot and asked the analyst for wholeness. And isn't that pretty much the same thing?

Mother Ann's "simplicity" is an exalted virtue, a kind of mystical oneness within and with God. It is a state for which many of us yearn because it seems to promise release from conflict—from the inner divisions that set us at war with ourselves and with others who reflect feared or hated parts of ourselves. The Shakers wisely connect simplicity with humility—earth-consciousness (humus = earth). We do not strive for simplicity; we bend to it. We do not achieve it; we turn toward it as in this Shaker hymn.

'Tis a gift to be simple
'Tis a gift to be free
'Tis a gift to come round where we ought to be
And when we find ourselves in the place just right
'Twill be in the Valley of Love and Delight.

When true simplicity is gained

To bow and to bend we will not be afraid.
To turn, to turn will be our delight
Till by turning, turning, we come round right.

Simplicity is not, as Mother Ann said, impossible, but it is, as she indicated, a gift to the humble. Simplicity does not come to us from the attempt to be like God, but rather from our realization that we are of earth. That we *are* earth. And earth is one only in its multiplicity. It is, as Gerard Manley Hopkins told us, pied. Dappled. "Swift, slow; sweet, sour; adazzle, dim." To find who we are we need to turn to everything, bowing and bending to earth. Each of us is a universe at the same time as each is a particle of a universe. All particles within us and all around us are connected. The oneness is of gay multiplicity, but it cannot be experienced unless we bend to it, turn to it. The fullness of life is to welcome the many, and, paradoxically, to welcome the many is to become simple and whole.

The welcoming is both to the many within and to the many outside of ourselves. The simplicity consists in being gifted to experience the many, not as objects to my subject but as particles of the whole, of which I, too, am a particle. We might say that the entire universe is one infinite organism, of which God is the soul, infusing and containing all its multiplicity in a pure oneness. It is not trying to be God that makes me simple but finding "the place just right," being in harmony with earth, with creation.

"Getting it together," even "getting myself together," is not my business. Allowing each part to find its place, to know itself, is my responsibility.

Only by welcoming the many can we finally become unselfcentered and be gifted with simplicity. We will never "get ourselves together," as a final solution to our wholeness or identity, for each of us is complete only as a part of something far larger— something ultimate. But we can bend and turn and find the place just right for the many within our own souls and for the multiplicity of all creation, of which we are a part. All of it comes together in God.

PSYCHIC DIFFERENTIATION

Most adult women need to begin with the many within them. If we look, most of us will find, tangled up in our psyches, numerous facets of our selves, more or less powerful, any of which can take over the whole personality in a given situation. How often have we reflected to ourselves, after a particularly emotional moment, "I acted like a child," or "I was behaving just like my mother!" At times we do not know what has possession of us. And that is what it feels like. Possession.

One woman who was a client of mine would be overtaken by a debilitating anxiety that would explode into violent anger. The only thing she knew about the source of the possession was that it felt like a black widow spider attached to her back. When this emotion came upon her, she would hunch up her shoulders and twist her head as though to get rid of some actual creature. She would whimper as though it were stinging her, and finally she would erupt in anger. After the episode she felt connections with her mother, but she could not locate anything actual that her mother might have done to cause such a strong reaction within her.

Often we must undertake intense psychic searches to find the facet of the personality that takes over in anxious or angry situations. Another client, a woman who was physically abused in her childhood and abandoned by her mother, imaged herself looking for the child she was before the abuse. She found herself walking along a road with a kind old woman who guided her to a large old house that seemed to be a museum. The old woman gave her a key and indicated that what she was looking for was inside. All at once she was alone. She looked at the key and began to try the doors to the house. The key fit into a small cellar door at the rear. Opening it, she found herself at the top of a long spiral stair leading down. As she descended she encountered seven more doors, which she unlocked. Finally she found herself at the entrance to what seemed to be a child's playhouse. The key fit. When she opened the door, she saw, huddled in a corner, the child she had been.

Walt Whitman said in "Song of Myself," "Do I contradict myself? Very well then I contradict myself. . . .(I am large, I contain multitudes.)"[1] I was often reminded of his words by a young woman with a chronic illness who came to me asking to find some meaning for her life. She experienced herself as disgusting, valueless, and teetering on the edge of despair. As I listened to her at our first session, I could not escape the impression that she was very hard on herself. Her body was stiff, her eyes glassy and protective. She seemed quite self-conscious and out of place in the space she occupied. Out of our conversation a picture of her life began to develop. She had grown up in a small southern town, the eldest daughter of a prominent businessman. Her father left the family when she was twelve years old and married a young dancer. She and her only sister were left with their mother, a strong, exacting, and dominant woman.

My client, whom I shall call Janice, carried a lot of responsibility, feeling a need to fill the emptiness left in her mother's life by the absence of her father—a task she could never accomplish. Her mother became the primary focus of her life. She said she "put Mom on a pedestal," and although she experienced some adolescent rebellion, she still believed that "Mom is always right about me." When she was a junior in high school, she found refuge from the intensity of her family life in participation in drama and the arts. Now, at twenty-one years of age, she considered that period of dramatic involvement the happiest time of her life.

One day when she was eighteen, she experienced her first epileptic seizure, which she described as deathly nauseating and embarrassing. To be out of control, not perfect, seemed worse than any affliction she could imagine. She identified herself now as an "epileptic slob" who could never live up to the ideal set by her mother. She was beginning to find that long-term relationships were difficult for her and that periods of depression and isolation from others were increasing.

My reason for highlighting Janice is that when she came to me I believe she had narrowed the scope of her identity to one facet—that of the epileptic. She found that persona debilitating. She felt her "being" to be an embarrassment. Janice was dangerously close to ending her life unless she could widen her sense of herself and welcome the many within.

I suggested to her that she imagine a round table at the center of herself. Sitting there, interacting with one another, were all the various facets of herself. I gave her some suggestions of facets (or faces) of inner persons: the mother, the child, the father, the student. At first she could see only three clearly: two mothers—one a great, good mother and the other a powerful and mean mother—and a little girl. Other persons were at the table, but they seemed like ghosts, their identities indistinguishable.

I suggested to her that she attempt to draw the round table and its people as a preparation for our next meeting. The next week she came back with a large diagram in which she identified the two primary centers of focus: a constellation of "good mother–little child–bad mother" and the "ego." The mother-child constellation was in a kind of tyrannical control. She had internalized and split the image of her dominant mother, capturing the child part of her psyche between the nurturing and demanding sides.

Janice had also named her "ghosts": father, lover-romantic, perfectionist, domestic, organizer, intellectual, and slob. But she drew these images as faint, with vague boundaries, and colorless.

As the weeks progressed, Janice continued to diagram until she was presenting numerous images in vivid color engaged in complex and always changing relationship with one another. An Amazon showed up and, joining with the ego and the little child, did battle with the bad mother and the perfectionist. The slob began to appear as not so bad after all and lent unique and helpful energies to the magnificent inner drama.

As Janice explored the rich dimensions of her soul, she also began to develop greater confidence for living. She chose to begin a university postgraduate program, became politically involved, and broadened the scope of her social contacts. It was a relaxed and comfortable young woman who left me after fourteen sessions to attend university in another state.

About six weeks after her departure, I received a letter from Janice that included a final diagram. She explained that she was having a great time, being successful in her classes, making friends, and volunteering time in a political party headquarters. She described some anxiety in dealing with her advisor, who seemed to pay no attention to her. But she recognized her anxiety and was seeing it as a part of the lie of the "dominant mother." I noticed on her diagram that this part of herself was now called "anxious Annie." She had infused a little humor into the mother complex, a move that would surely diffuse its power. The "ego" remained well defined and developed. The Amazon looked to be having fun, infusing energy into the "little child" and the "little professor." A "dancing Doris," "unflappable cucumber," and the "slob" were right there as backups in case the "perfectionist" (who is missing from the diagram for the first time) should reappear. "Fearless Frieda" had connected herself to the "friend," strengthening Janice's social sense and her ability to be intimate. The "lover-romantic" was now connected with the "friend" as well and was developing into something new that was not yet named. The feminine artist had joined a grouping of masculine energies, no doubt infusing them with more creative power.

Janice was happy. She had gone from a stiff, one-dimensional young woman on the edge of despair to a woman with a rich character who understood the energies within herself and was able to deal with them in the real situations of her life. She no longer thought of herself as an "epileptic slob"; rather, she welcomed the "slob" within as a necessary facet of herself. Welcoming the many within herself had given her hope for a more full and meaningful life, and energy to live that life creatively.

Because Janice was in transition from adolescence to young adulthood, the process of differentiating and welcoming the many within herself was relatively simple. Her developmental task centered on formation of identity, a task that focuses primarily on primacy of the ego. When she came to me, the process of ego development had been frustrated by her attempts to cope with her epilepsy, combined with the internalized admonitions of her mother that she be perfect. Our work together was brief and successful because of its relative simplicity.

When women are older than Janice, the process can take a lot longer and can produce hundreds of diagrams. The task, rather than being ego-centered, proceeds toward integration of the many facets in the self. Even beyond self-integration, we work toward the enlivening of soul in relation to the Ultimate Holy One.

Janice was fortunate to have been prodded by her physical condition to begin the process of welcoming the many as early in life as she did. Most contemporary women are in their mid-thirties to early fifties before some contingency of their lives leaves them in severe psychic pain that prompts them to seek healing, clarity, or meaning. The process for the older woman needs to begin precisely where Janice's did: with the development of ego. However, ego development is only the first step with women past thirty. They need to advance further to self-integration and to body-soul awareness in relationship to God.

THE "I AM" EXPERIENCE

When the process of ego development comes later in life, women often experience tremendous disruption in their living situations. The ego's necessary cry, "I am who I am," can lead women to radical changes in life-style. For example, if a woman marries, or enters a religious community, before the ego is differentiated from the inner child or the inner parent or some other powerful facet of the psyche, she may later experience herself controlled by her marriage partner, or her religious community, in ways she does not understand. Although at the beginning of her commitment she may have felt secure in following the promptings of these inner forces, as the ego claims its separate identity a spirit of rebellion takes over. She experiences an inner war, but she tends to act it out on the person or people to whom she is now committed.

If she has been in the control of a parenting complex whose admonition is "Take care of everything," her developing ego is likely to take a stand against taking care. If the admonition comes from a different source—the child, for instance: "Take care of me,"—her ego is likely to declare, "Leave me alone. I will take care of myself." The spouse she married for his ability to set limits for her because her parents were inconsistent now hears her say, "I will not do as you say. From now on, I will do as *I* think best." The spouse she married because he needed her—she having been taught that she was only meaningful when taking care of others—now hears her proclaim, "No more! You are responsible for yourself. I cannot take care of you. I have no responsibility for you. My responsibility is to myself!"

When women come to me as clients during this confusing time, they often say, "I really love my husband [my religious community] but he suffocates me. If I continue the relationship as it is, I will die. I cannot sacrifice myself so that he [they] might live." One thirty-five-year-old woman dreamed that she needed to commit suicide so that her husband could live. She came to me filled with angry ego power. "I will not do it! I will not die so that he can live! *I* will be! *I* will live!"

This is a time of family disruption, sometimes of divorce. Sisters leave their religious communities. The development of ego is absolutely necessary. The danger is that women will get stuck there. Ideally, ego development would take place before any life commitment would be made. In a society that traditionally keeps females in a dependent and subservient position the ideal has rarely happened. Perhaps in the future this problem will be greatly minimized because the social system is becoming more and more accepting of young women with strong egos. But this is a transitional time. Women in mid-life are awakening to what they missed in their development, claiming it, and finding themselves enraged that the times were against them before. Now there is so much to make up. There is so much disruption to endure.

In the welcoming of the many, the first to be welcomed must be the ego—the "I am." There can be no welcoming without the "I." For some of us, those in mid-life, this initial welcoming will require regression and the disruption that often accompanies regression. We will be called selfish, angry women. We will be accused of not caring for our families. We will be blamed for the chaos of divorce. We will hear "I told you so" when we come home exhausted from attempts to reeducate ourselves, to find a job, or to adjust to the professional life–family life balancing act. We will seek out other women who are trying to find the solid ground of "I," the beginning place out of which to evolve a soul. We will form networks and support groups. We will try to teach ourselves that this "selfish" thing we are doing is necessary and good. We will be haunted by the voices of the past, the condemning voices within. We will begin the process of welcoming the many.

I have found in working with women who are experiencing this process that they cannot think of ego development as a first step in a process or as a transition. Because we women have been taught so well that "living for ourselves" is selfish and evil, we seem to need all our energy and concentration to allow our egos to emerge. We seem to need to experience ego emergence as an end in itself. We gather up all our energy to overthrow the admonitions against selfishness that kept us from becoming persons in our own right. Those admonitions are not appropriate for one who has no "I," no ego on which to center.

The "I am" experience often comes upon a woman with a numinosity that gives it spiritual power. Conviction follows. On the force of this conviction some women have let go of their entire past to construct for themselves radically new personalities and life-styles. The stakes are higher at mid-life than when we are in our early twenties. The letting go can feel outrageous.

If we can endure this transformation without clinging to the new and becoming trapped in it as we were in the old, the development will continue. The ego is only the first of many to be welcomed. After proclaiming "I am," we can go on within our psyches to encounter multitudes.

My own "I am" experience came to me when I was thirty-one years of age and struggling with the decision of whether or not to remain in the religious community of which I had been a member for fourteen years. For the past two years I had been throwing myself into community renewal efforts, trying to prove to myself and to others that I belonged. However, my giving of myself to the community did not have the effect I wanted. Instead, I felt increasingly exhausted and empty. I felt like nobody.

One night the struggle became critical. I reasoned: "My past two years have showed me that no amount of commitment to religious community will relieve me of this nothingness. The more I give myself, the more nothing I become. If I stay, I will lose myself entirely. On the other hand, the only thing I know about myself is that I am a sister. I have been a sister since I was a child, having entered the community at seventeen years of age. If I leave, I will no longer be a sister. I will be nothing. No matter what I do, I end up being nothing. Since I am nothing anyway, I may as well kill myself." Something in me countered immediately with "You can't kill yourself. You'll go to hell!" I answered back: "I owe it to myself to consider it as an option."

All at once I felt too tired to think anymore. I lay back on my bed and fell into a deep sleep that lasted the entire night. I awoke to the sun and a bird singing outside the window. From deep within me came the words of the Easter Mass, "I am risen and I am still with you." Then echoing loudly throughout my entire being I kept hearing the words *I am! I am! I am!* Instinctively I knew that I was not nothing. I knew that leaving religious community or staying did not matter so much as that I am. I left two days later. And I am.

The ego, fully welcomed and no longer fearful of suppression, becomes in her turn a welcoming agent. Ego-centeredness results not from a too-strong ego but from one that is so weak that it must focus constantly on itself in order not to fade into nothingness from lack of concentration or not to be trampled on and shamed by the world outside. When the ego is weak, all our psychic energy seems to need to be engaged there. Little or nothing is left over either for the enhancement of our own characters or for a free and generous welcoming of people in the human community whose needs cry out to us.

This is not to say that people with poorly developed egos cannot help others. In fact, women have done it for centuries in cultures, like our own, that keep us in subservient positions. Often, however, the helping is done to prove our worth. We need to be needed in order to be. And the result to us is psychic exhaustion in mid-life, if not sooner. We find we have given everything away; we have given ourselves away, and nothing remains but a mask formed in the image of what others have wanted us to be. The emptiness, the nothingness of our souls terrifies us. Then comes the despair or the rebellion and, at last, the welcoming of the ego, the "I Am" experience.

Only after "I am" is true service, true giving, real generosity possible. We begin to sense the spheres of welcome within, which prepare us, by a total acceptance of self, to welcome the world.

CHAPTER 11

Spheres of Welcome

The spheres of welcome in our selves are three: the body, the soul, and the spirit. These spheres must be pictured not as separate from each other but as concentric globes of color overlapping and mingling: the red-orange of the body, the yellow-green of the soul, and the blue-violet of the spirit. Each influences the others; none is complete alone.

WELCOMING BODY

The body is not simply matter, not simply flesh; it is, rather, the focused manifestation of psychic processes. Body is the aspect of the self that participates in the materiality of the universe and connects the microcosm within to the macrocosm without. As embodied consciousness we are, indeed, cosmic creatures, made of the very stuff of the stars. We never cease to be; we are only transformed in the continuous cycle of matter and energy.

Body is the sphere of sense, instinct, and feeling. As body-persons we sense our intimate connections with earth. If we develop our sense life and keep it sharp, we benefit from this earth connection enormously. We find in ourselves a kinship with earth, and our bodies resonate with her movement: the calming rhythm of ocean waves, the cycles of the moon, the ebb and flow of the tides, the high and low pressures of the winds and currents of air. We are thrilled and terrified in our very flesh by the rush of spring floods, the tearing of earthquakes, the erupting of volcanos. We sense our wholeness with everything on summer nights, lying on the cool grass, engulfed by the never-ending night and its birthgiving stars.

Each of us senses in earth what is most life-giving to us as individuals. Lena gardens. She doesn't think about it; she only lets herself feel her oneness with the life-giving loam as she plants, waters, and tends her flowers and herbs. She senses simultaneous coming to life within her self. Margaret climbs rocks; she feels their power and stability; she senses her own strength and the ability to conquer fear. JoAnn walks in the woods; her senses open to receive the communication of birds, stones, trees. When she rests against a giant oak, she thanks it for its kindness in kinship.

It is with the sphere of body that we sense danger in the earth. We feel disharmony. Imbalance within ourselves and outside of ourselves gives rise to dis-ease and unhealthiness. Imbalance in technology and disturbance of natural rhythms creates pollution in the earth and in the body. If we are sensible, we restore harmony. If we block our sense of dis-ease, the material world becomes more dis-ordered.

Dharma, the element of balance and justice in religions of the East, is violated by the blockage of our sense of earth and body. World begins to fall apart. Healing is needed, therapy is needed. Our word *therapy* comes from the eastern root *dhar*, the same as that for dharma. The only therapy for a diseased earth or body is the restoration of balance and order, a returning to our senses. This is humility again. A turning to the earth, "till by turning, turning, we come round right."

Body is the sphere of instinct. Primitive human beings needed to be aware of danger within the first few seconds of an encounter to take the action necessary for survival. Instinct triggered the fight-or-flight mechanism and the person reacted. Like the doe who bounds into the forest at the sound of the hunter's foot landing on dry twigs, a human being also feels an almost immediate quickening in the body at the sight or sound of danger. The heart beats faster; the mouth becomes dry; arms and legs seem poised and energized for action. We ignore this reaction at our peril.

Instinct is an unconscious reaction. We do not reason about it. Our instinctual responses may not even be based on reasonable data, as we may find when we later pause to analyze them.

Nevertheless, those responses seem necessary at the time. Instinct differs from those habitual responses built up over time because of repeated experience. For example, if I had been beaten by my father during my childhood and then by my husband as an adult, I might experience a consistent and intense fight-or-flight reaction whenever I encountered any man. But this would be habit, not instinct.

There is a preconsciousness to instinct. Instinct's energy warns us of danger or attracts us to what is life-giving. It then impels us toward what is for our body's good. In our culture and time we have become so "reasonable" that we often miss instinctual reactions in everyday affairs—or we disregard them as foolish. An example occurs to me from my own recent experience.

I had been at a conference during which I met a woman who was a well-known lecturer on women's issues. During the time of the conference, I spoke with her only once, at the moment of introduction. After that I instinctively kept my distance, hardly noticing and not caring at all that there was no communication between us. I neither thought about it nor questioned it.

Some weeks later I received a phone call from her. She asked if I would codirect a workshop with her. Overlooking a mild feeling of discomfort at the base of my spine and in my belly, I suggested we meet for lunch to get to know one another and determine if we could work together. Again, at the luncheon meeting, I felt the discomfort—now a kind of strong repellency. As we talked I kept looking for some reason to back up what I was sensing. There seemed to be none. Our ideas on both content and methodology for the workshop were consistent. I said I would let her know my decision in the next two weeks.

It was so easy to put off calling her that three weeks passed before I took myself in hand one day and said, "Christin, this is just ridiculous! Call the woman and accept!" I did. But the plans didn't work out. I prepared for my part in the workshop—talks, groups, rituals—but just a few days before it was to take place, she sent a letter changing the entire program. I was furious—not only with her for unilaterally changing what was supposed to have been a plan created by the two of us, but also with myself for not following my instincts.

Although it is probably not wise to follow our instincts without question, it is even more foolish to ignore them completely. At the very least, an instinctual reaction should give us a pause signal. If the instinct does not make rational sense, wait. Listen. Feel. Only after we become conscious of its origin, of what is stimulating the reaction, do we dare to decide whether or not to override it. If I had listened to my instincts, I still could have codirected the workshop, but I would have exercised more caution in my dealings with this woman. I would have called her to account regularly during the months of planning. I would have known that my greatest output of energy would have had to be in maintaining clear and precise communication between the two of us.

We must never override instinct with reason until we have determined why the instinct has risen up within us. Instinct, like sensation, must be welcomed.

Finally, body is the sphere of feeling. In the concentric sphere metaphor, feeling would be the orange that is turning into gold, just at the threshold of and even mingling with soul. Feeling reaches into sensation and instinct, connecting them and sorting them out into meaningful response. Feeling gives a name to the response: love, joy, enthusiasm, anger, fear, desire. It focuses the response and assigns value to it.

There are people who have not welcomed feeling or who have lost the ability to feel. Jane is a client who came to me with just that concern. She was beginning to experience marital problems because she had no feeling in her relationship to her spouse. Instead, she followed precise patterns of learned behavior in every facet of her life. This carefully constructed drama served her well for much of her youthful life, but now, after several years of marriage, her spouse wanted more. He complained that something was missing in her, something he called feeling.

Jane found the whole realm of feeling a mystery. She simply could not fathom how people did it: how they managed to feel when another person was hurt, to feel what an appropriate birthday gift might be—even to experience a feeling of celebration that might lead to remembering someone's birthday. She had forgotten her spouse's last birthday—much to his distress and her consternation over the fuss. In our initial sessions Jane sat tapping her foot and speaking in monosyllabic responses to my questions. Her face remained passive and masklike. She did explain that she was coming to me to learn to feel—to find out why she could not feel and to remedy the situation.

As time went on and Jane began to trust me more, she revealed some of her story. Her childhood was dominated by an extremely overprotective mother and a mostly absent father. She began very early protecting her mother from worry, a task which proved impossible because the less trouble Jane got into, the smaller were the incidents her mother blew out of proportion to maintain her worrying stance. Jane's increasing attempts to protect mother, and her consistent failure to be able to succeed in that task, finally led to a shutdown of her personality. She learned the drama of pleasing mother but at the same time built strong walls against the inevitable failure. No feeling could be permitted, for it was sure to be abused.

Jane claimed to have only one memory of the experience of feeling. It happened in high school when she fell in love with a boy who was captain of the football team. For almost a year they dated and even discussed marriage. Then without warning he left her and began to date someone else. When Jane finally did marry, it was to a man with feeling enough for both of them, or so she thought. As it turned out, he was much like her mother in that he attempted to control her by his own needs. Now his need was for her to feel, and she experienced herself caught in a strong double bind.

Only with the threat of divorce did Jane's barrier to feeling break. Divorce would be the ultimate failure. She sat in agonized silence. Finally she said, very softly, "All these years I have tried to be what other people wanted me to be; first my mother, now my spouse—even my boss, my friends, everybody. I act. But underneath the act there is nothing. There really is no me. Where I am supposed to be is only a gigantic emptiness. I am nothing." Then she began to cry. "I feel so alone. I cannot even tell my spouse; I do not feel I can trust him." She continued to weep during the rest of our time together that day. But she had broken through to the reservoir of feeling, and despite the pain, or perhaps because of it, her life as herself had begun.

Feeling appears to be strongly connected with sensation and instinct, perhaps receiving its propelling energy from them. Instinct, in the presence of danger, triggers the feeling of fear and/ or anger. When the body is hungry, instinct seeks nourishment and triggers feelings of pleasure over imminent fulfillment. If parts of our bodies have become numb to sensation, we find that certain feelings cannot be released. Bioenergetic therapists work with the body to help it let go of stored-up and calcified energy.

A former client of mine had experienced the loss of her husband to cancer very soon after the death of her child. To keep her life functional and herself able to care for her other children, she grieved moderately and then stopped. By the time she came to see me, some five years later, she could not raise the feelings of loss; a kind of paralysis and malaise had taken her over. She had difficulty making any decisions for herself or feeling pleased with anything she accomplished. My work with her was moderately helpful but did not seem to reach the deepest pain. Finally she agreed to seeing a bioenergetics therapist, who worked exclusively with her body, finding those places in her shoulders, her belly, and her throat where the energy was paralyzed and the feeling was stuck. When the body was relaxed, the sensation came back and the feelings of pain and grief were finally released.

During our "Womanbody, Womansoul" workshops, Suzanne Swanson and I witness the same connections between sensation and feeling. During a guided meditation we suggest that each woman allow a sphere of pure energy and light to enter her body and travel slowly through every part. There has been no woman who has participated in this exercise who has not reported some numbness in her body at some point—thighs, stomach, throat, and so on. The energy will stop there, will be blocked, will need to find an alternate route. In the ensuing discussion we find a strong correlation between the blocked sensing in the body and pent-up feelings. We have also found that the guided imagery can be a powerful way to bring the dead senses back to life and restore energy to the feelings.

WELCOMING SOUL

In guided imagery we begin to enter upon the sphere of the soul. Soul gives meaning to life. It is not a separate entity from body; rather, it expands the body's awareness beyond its spatial limits through a process of ever-increasing consciousness. In soul, instinct expands to become intuition; sense expands into mystic awareness; and feeling joins with thinking to become wisdom. While body's sense, instinct, and feeling respond directly to the reality at hand, soul's intuition, mystic awareness, and wisdom respond also to that reality's origins and potential for future unfolding, as well as to its value and meaning. Soul integrates analytical thought with intuitive thought, joins these with mystic awareness and perceives reality analogically, operating in the realm of images.

Images are either psychic or archetypal, that is, originating out of the depths of one's own soul or out of the vast reservoir of the "collective unconscious." Psychic images carry the energy of my personal history of experience transformed into meaningful symbol. Archetypal images carry the energy of the collective life history of this planet and transmit a kind of power that I experience as both my own and greater than myself—a power that fills me with fascination and awe. Although the soul is the receptor of the archetypal image, it must never identify with it, for the collective energy is so beyond an individual's capacity for containment that identification with an archtype destroys the individual. We witness this in advanced mental illness when a person believes himself or herself to *be* Christ or Hitler or the Great Mother or Kali.

The processes of soul are dreams, visions, meditative states, and ritual. All the great works of humankind—works of art, science, religion, and technology—arise from the soul or they do not last and may even be destructive. We cannot prevent the soul from producing, and this is both our glory and our shame. For if we repress the images of the soul, if we refuse the intuition, mysticism, and wisdom the soul gives rise to, then the repressed energy sours, ferments, and finally breaks through in a production of "evil." We find we have no power over this breakthrough and are unconscious of it until we produce it. This production of "evil" happens at the level of the individual and also at the level of the community. Jung believed that Nazism was the breakthrough of repressed archetypes in the German people. Present thinkers speculate that our repression of soul on a global level in contemporary times could result in nuclear holocaust.

So the processes of soul need to be welcomed not only to assure the continued evolution of our human being but to prevent our ultimate destruction of ourselves. Intuition, as the most primary of these processes, can be described as an eruption into consciousness of an idea or image from the unconscious. We experience a kind of wholeness about the idea because we perceive in it both the seed of its origin and the vision of its completion. It is in the present but for the future. As such it is compelling and draws us into a vision for life beyond our personal limits at present.

A friend of mine once described an intuitive student of hers in a manner so graphic I have never forgotten it: "Her soul is like a deep well. Presented with a mystery of life, she plunges instantaneously into the depths and surfaces with a treasure of insight."

Because our intellectual community in recent centuries, since the scientific revolution, has emphasized the demonstrable and the analytical, the intuitive processes have not enjoyed the respect due to them. In fact, intuition has been denigrated and trivialized in many circles as being flighty and unsubstantiated. This is changing. Even science has now reached the limits of its ability to analyze and demonstrate, working as it does with "tendencies" in the microcosmic world. Scientists tell us, for example, that the microcosm produced the macrocosm in a manner we can only grasp intuitively; they calculate that the entire universe, the inconceivable vastness of the cosmos, has grown and continues to grow out of a region billions of times smaller than one proton.

What could such a "region" be? Certainly not matter as we know it. Certainly not even space as we know it. Not something measurable. Perhaps something like a word. "In the beginning was the Word." Here we have mystery. I think it was Maslow who claimed somewhere in his writings that science is what we can know about the Mystery. Mystery is the soul's realm; intuition is the way we perceive it.

Mysticism is participation in the Mystery. If intuition is a mode of perception, a way of knowing, then mysticism is a way of loving reality in its infinite dimensions. Though mysticism is related to sensation, it differs from it in that sensation is one-dimensional and symbiotic. It participates in reality right here and now as that reality manifests itself to the senses. It vibrates and flows with that reality and feels one with it. In religious experience sensation puts us in touch with the immanent holiness. Mysticism adds the dimensions of origin and future fulfillment, going beyond what is available to the senses to participate in a transcendent holiness. It is the soul's yearning to love Ultimate Reality. Mysticism's tendency is not to seek to know but to seek to be united.

Mystic consciousness becomes aware of images—visual, auditory, kinesthetic—rising from the depths of the unconscious and perhaps from beyond. It yearns toward these images—listening, waiting—not so much to learn something of Mystery as to be taken in by Mystery in a loving embrace. Knowing is a by-product of mysticism, but not its goal. The result of mystic experience is greater be-ing.

A woman who is a member of the Wisdom House creative worship community told of a mystic experience that happened during one of our rituals. We had spent about forty minutes in guided meditation, descending into the depths through the seven energy centers of body and soul, the chakras. It was a kind of "descent to the Goddess." When this woman reached the glowing red space of the root chakra—the space of earth and beginning, of primal creation—she experienced herself becoming a kind of world tree. Her roots reached deep into the universe, and she felt herself rising up, strong and very large. Her branches touched the stars to umbrella the world. Love for and union with Ultimate Reality overwhelmed her and produced in her a deep affection for the community and a desire to share that love and union with us. There seemed to be in her no striving to "know" the meaning of this vision; there was only the acceptance of an infusion of love and a gentle desire to share that love with others.

Mystic images communicate a kind of being. We feel them as transformational and intensely mysterious. They are almost never predictable, nor do they take expected forms. A colleague of mine related the story of an American Indian woman who had suffered terrible abuse throughout her life and who, in recent years, had undergone numerous surgeries to remove diseased parts of her body. She had prayed and prayed to Christ to heal her, with no success.

In a guided mediation my colleague led her to the top of a mountain to encounter a wisdom figure. The woman expected to find Christ there but did not. Instead, a man with the head of an eagle waited for her. She fought the image, but he seemed so filled with strength, light, and comfort that she finally allowed herself to be embraced by him. In that embrace she received an infusion of strength, healing, and love that so transformed her in body and soul that she experienced measurable improvement in her health.

Since she was Christian, the appearance of a Native American image of God surprised and confused her. But she must have needed to welcome facets of her soul that could participate in divine manifestations consistent with her racial history and traditions. Any image of God is simply an image. Mystic consciousness ultimately transcends images, participating in the Ultimate Ground from which all images proceed.

WELCOMING SPIRIT

This Ultimate Ground is the sphere of spirit. In spirit the self becomes transpersonal, and the activity of life is belief. Christ manifests this sphere in all the dimensions of his being: in his Incarnation, in the true Christian community, and in the fulfillment of the universe in the Cosmic Christ. Christ is the manifestation of wisdom—the soul's union of knowing and loving—in each of us. Christ is the Incarnation of the Wisdom of God, Sophia, in the world. As such, Christ unites feminine and masculine, individual and universal, and becomes the only name by which we can be saved.

In the Wisdom of Christ, soul and body are united in spirit. The Christ is the one who dared the descent into body, becoming incarnate, taking on everything that is earth, completing creation in that incarnate body. Wisdom—Sophia—is she who plays creation into being. Wisdom is the divine process of creation, materializing the infinite knowing and loving of God. Solomon tells us:

In [Wisdom] is a spirit
    intelligent, holy, unique,
Manifold, subtle, agile,
    clear, unstained, certain,
Not baneful, loving the good, keen,
    unhampered, beneficent, kindly,
Firm, secure, tranquil,
    all-powerful, all-seeing,
And pervading all spirits,
        though they be intelligent, pure and
            very subtle.
For Wisdom is mobile beyond all motion
    and she penetrates and pervades all
        things by reason of her purity.
For she is an aura of the might of God
    and a pure effusion of the glory of the
Almighty;
        therefore nought that is sullied enters into her.
For she is the refulgence of eternal light,
    the spotless mirror of the power of God,
    the image of his goodness.
And she, who is one, can do all things,
    and renews everything while herself perduring;
And passing into holy souls from age to age,
    she produces friends of God and prophets.
For there is nought God loves, be it not
    one who dwells with Wisdom.
For she is fairer than the sun
    and surpasses every constellation of the stars.
Compared to light, she takes precedence;
    for that, indeed, night supplants,
    but wickedness prevails not over Wisdom.
Indeed, she reaches from end to end mightily
    and governs all things well.

                            (Wisdom 7:22–8:1 NAB)

This divine Lady Wisdom reached into the woman's womb
to be enfleshed as the Christ. In the Christ there is no exclusively
male or female. Jesus was the masculine embodiment of the feminine Lady Sophia, Divine Wisdom. When we welcome the
Christ within, we welcome a wholeness of being beyond our
imagining. We welcome a power and a humanness so complete
and so one with the Ultimate Holy Being that we cannot grasp

the mystery of it and can only respond in faith. As the depths of the mystery of what we are welcoming become clearer to us, our lives ignite in an ecstasy of welcome for all that is within ourselves, no matter how imperfect or broken we had previously regarded it. And we feel a pouring out of welcome for all of earth and her inhabitants, no matter their weakness or their sin.

This spirit of welcome, the wisdom of welcoming, becomes the hallmark of Christianity as well as its final judgment. Judgment means a sorting out, a differentiating, a setting apart of that which fits the pattern of creative wisdom from that which does not. Before Vatican II, Roman Catholics began every mass with a prayer for such judgment: "Júdica me, Deus, et discérne causam meam de gente non sancta:" "Judge me, O God, and distinguish my cause against what is not holy" (Psalm 42).

In the collection of parables about judgment in the Gospel of St. Matthew, we are instructed to be watchful and conscious, to be individuated and industrious, and to bring the gifts of our life to their fulfillment. But the last judgment, which determines whether or not we have truly become participants in the creative process, joining the human and divine in a oneness of simplicity, is a judgment of welcoming.

"Come. You have my Father's blessing." This is the Christ, incarnation of Sophia, the divine feminine Wisdom, who speaks. The Divine Feminine calls and receives; the Divine Masculine blesses.

" 'Inherit the [reign] prepared for you from the creation of the world. For I was hungry and you gave me food, I was thirsty and you gave me drink. I was a stranger and you welcomed me, naked and you clothed me. I was ill and you comforted me, in prison and you came to visit me.' Then the just will ask him: 'Lord, when did we see you hungry and feed you or see you thirsty and give you drink? When did we welcome you away from home or clothe you in your nakedness? When did we visit you when you were ill or in prison?' The [Christ] will answer them: 'I assure you, as often as you did it for one of my least brothers [or sisters], you did it for me.' "

(Matthew 25:34–40 NAB)

A spirituality of welcoming the many combines the three spheres—body, soul, and spirit—and opens to the hungry, the thirsty, the stranger, the naked, the sick, and the imprisoned. When we can welcome the many in our bodies, through our sensation, our instinct, and our feeling, when we can welcome

the many in our souls, through our images, then we may be able
to welcome the Christ in all the guises of Wisdom manifest in
creation.

> The day of my spiritual awakening
> was the day I saw
> and knew I saw
> all things in God
> and God
> in all things.[1]

So declares the thirteenth-century mystic, Mechtild of Magdeburg. Those the embrace of whom involves us in the embrace
of the Christ live in all spheres of welcome. Each of us is hungry
in body and in soul. Each is a stranger, naked, sick, imprisoned.
Each is thirsty. Spirituality requires us to ask of our own selves:
What in me is hungry? How do I thirst? How have I become a
stranger? To what am I naked? What is my sickness? What parts
of me are imprisoned?

Only when we are willing to engage in the process of welcoming all that is within, and welcome those many facets of self
as manifestations of grace, can we say we are engaging in true
spirituality. But it does not stop there. When what is hungry in
my bodysoul is recognized and respected, then I will be able to
feel the hunger of others and reach out to them in compassion.
I will not *need* others to be needy to give me a reason for being;
rather, I will overflow with welcoming because I will know that
my hunger and their hunger is one: the hunger of the Christ.
There is *one* who is thirsty, *one* who is a stranger, naked, sick,
and imprisoned. It is the Cosmic Christ, the Wisdom of all creation, moaning and struggling in a labor of birth. My pain is not
separate from yours, and ours is a world struggle. Refusal of
welcome is self-destruction, perhaps even destruction of the
world. I cannot refuse to welcome you without refusing myself,
without refusing the world, without refusing the Christ.

In the end we find simplicity. We welcome all being with the
humility of earth. We turn and bend to even what is weakest in
us, individually and collectively, and embrace it. And in that
embrace we find ourselves embraced by Incarnate Wisdom,
Christ/Sophia. For we are all one Body and the Body is God's.

CHAPTER 12

Whirling with Chaos

When I was a child in northern Minnesota, I delighted in walking alone at night. My feet would have to find their own way along the small town road, for my head would be tilted up toward the stars. The stars are brighter where no city lights drown them. In winter northern lights moved like immense curtains through the sky, mostly silver, but sometimes colored in greens, reds, and golds. I don't see them now, in the city; I know they are there but so delicate that the electric glow makes them invisible.

When I was a child, the night sky filled me with deep peace and security. Its beauty seemed eternal, as did the firmness of the earth beneath my feet. Standing upon earth, I wondered if everything above the grass were sky, and if I were, therefore, a part of the sky. At least my thoughts were. My desires were. I liked to sing, and I would make up songs to cast at the stars.

Still, I love the night sky and gaze upon it whenever I have the chance. In the city the stars are more difficult to see, but the large constellations are still there. In the city I do not walk alone, but I do take the moments from the house to the car, or while walking around the block in the summer with my spouse, to make my connections with the dance of the stars.

My mood is different. Lately, I have not been able to look at the sky without automatically breathing a prayer: "Please, Holy One, do not let us destroy this beauty!" I feel the earth upon which I stand, and it feels no longer eternal but enormously vulnerable. If there is no longer any earth, there will be no place to stand from which to see and dance with the sky. Continued

existence feels tentative, dependent on power-dominated people, on paranoid computers.

I stand surrounded by the night sky, feeling a burden of pain
for the fragility of this earth, and I love the sky and the earth
like one loving a person who is about to go to war, not knowing
whether that loved one will return. It makes me angry; and I
feel myself becoming just a little mad.

Cosmos and chaos both whirl in a never-ending cycle of
forming and fragmenting worlds. Each of us participates in the
whirling of the worlds—in the creativity and madness. We are,
simultaneously, coming into being and disintegrating—losing
the form of being we have known and becoming transformed.

Unless we are willing to whirl with the chaos, we can never
create. The Holy One breathed into the chaos, sent the Spirit to
whirl with its vast darkness, to begin the original creative process. Jesus entered his creative life of ministry through the wilderness (chaos). There he hoped to encounter the Spirit who
forms and transforms everything that is. Paradoxically he met
what we all meet in the whirling of chaos. Evil.

We cannot be creative without entering chaos. And we cannot enter into chaos without confronting evil. And the confrontation with evil can make us mad, or make us artists, reformers,
and saints.

But what is the "evil" we meet in today's whirling of worlds?
What is "madness"? What does it mean to go mad? What is sin
in our world today?

Recent women's literature often uses madness as a symbolic
event initiating women into reality. It is through madness that
the woman lets go of an order of being that is destructive to her,
that forms her into a kind of doll or puppet woman, that takes
away her natural being and makes her into something not-
woman.

In the pain of being no one, women seem driven to immerse
themselves in earth, either by increasing the flesh of their own
bodies, as Isabel does in Mary Gordon's Final Payments, or by
losing their bodies and souls in the chaos of nature itself. Such
is the woman's experience in Margaret Atwood's Surfacing. Pregnant and fearing the implications of parenthood, she journeys
far up in the Quebec wilderness to seek her own parent and the
reality of her womanself. The contrast between nature and the

superficiality of the culture to which she has conformed drives her to repudiate civilization as dangerous to her. She allows herself to dissolve into nature, to become animal, to become plant, to become earth itself. She goes mad, but the emerges alive.

What else, what else? Enough for a while. I sit down, wrapping myself in the blanket which is damp from the grass, my feet have gone cold. I will need other things, perhaps I can catch a bird or a fish, with my hands, that will be fair. Inside me it is growing, they take what they require, if I don't feed it it will absorb my teeth, bones, my hair will thin, come out in handfuls. But I put it there, I invoked it, the fur god with tail and horns, already forming. The mothers of gods, how do they feel, voices and light glaring from the belly, do they feel sick, dizzy? Pain squeezes my stomach, I bend, head pressed against knees.

Slowly I retrace the trail. Something has happened to my eyes, my feet are released, they alternate, several inches from the ground. I'm ice-clear, transparent, my bones and the child inside me showing through the green webs of my flesh, the ribs are shadows, the muscles jelly, the trees are like this too, they shimmer, their cores glow through the wood and bark.

The forest leaps upward, enormous, the way it was before they cut it, columns of sunlight frozen; the boulders float, melt, everything is made of water, even the rocks. In one of the languages there are no nouns, only verbs held for a longer moment.

The animals have no need for speech, why talk when you are a word

I lean against a tree, I am a tree leaning

I break out again into the bright sun and crumple, head against the ground

I am not an animal or a tree, I am the thing in which the trees and animals move and grow, I am a place[1]

In a world of mind and machines it seems to be madness for us to find our connections with body and with earth, madness not to conform. One of my clients was tried last week for the gross misdemeanor of destroying property. She had dug a grave in the earth where Honeywell, Inc., has constructed its buildings, within which to do research and produce weapons of destruction. Hers was an act of madness against a military-industrial establishment engaged in acts of madness against the earth itself. By her madness she sought to bring back sanity. By her nonconformity of protest against the established order, she sought to re-form and bring new creative order to society.

EVIL VS. THE DIVINE FOOL

Looking at the world today, I see two kinds of madness. One is the madness that leads to evil. It takes the "form" of creation and turns it against itself in a mal-formation, threatening the destruction of creation itself. So we have nuclear madness, the madness of pollution, the madness of a widening gulf between the rich and the poor—leading to the madness of starvation of whole peoples, the madness of warring for power over others, the madness of sexism, the madness of child abuse, the madness of deadening our souls to the yearning in life to continue the creative process. This is the madness that is evil, that is sin. When we conform to this malformation, we become sin. This is the sin of the world.

The other madness is that of the Divine Fool. It is the madness that refuses to conform to malformation. "In the eyes of the world," says the apostle, "we seem to be mad." This is the madness of the protester, of the artist, of the saint—of the one who is willing to appear de-formed in order to inform, reform, transform.

The Divine Fool dances with the stars. The Fool whirls in the center of chaos, holding the worlds together in cosmos. This whirling dance of folly, by which creation continues forming, draws into itself whatever serves the universe and deflects evil, flinging it into nothingness.

The Fool dis-illusions. When the maker of madness that destroys the world gazes with serious face into the contrary face of the Fool, the illusion of respectability dissolves. The madness of the Fool demonstrates the deformities of whatever is evil in the times. We then must choose: the present illusory form the world takes, or the Fool. We either conform to the destructive madness of a malformed order of being or experience the "folly" of a Divine Madness in the service of creation—our own and that of a world needing to be transformed.

On Good Friday I went to visit Addie in the locked intensive care unit of a local psychiatric hospital. When I came into her room, she was sleeping on one of the five beds. Each bed was bolted to the floor, as were the five small bedside tables. Aside from these pieces of furniture, the room was bare, constructed to reduce the risk of a patient's causing herself harm.

Even after Addie awoke, she seemed dreamy. Massive doses of medication kept her almost immobile, even though the drugs did not eliminate the voices that taunted her to take her life. I sat with her. She held my hand as if I were a kind of lifeline. She studied my face and searched my eyes. She talked about the voices, about death, and questioned the sanity of remaining alive. I held her slender, dark hand and wondered about how we waste our riches—the people we live alongside. Mostly we were silent, keeping a kind of vigil of the soul, mourning a life being poured out for what seemed meaningless, hoping and waiting for a kind of resurrection.

In Addie I saw an image of the madness of a society in which children can be raped, abandoned, shamed. In her beautiful black face I saw the dark goddess, the "Stranger of God"—a drugged divinity, feared and rejected. She could hear the voices plotting her destruction. It was not her madness, it was ours that was killing her. There was not even honor in being an image; she was not a hero, not a saint. She was just a nineteen-year-old black girl whom society had failed. But she was WomanChrist that Good Friday.

Madness becomes evil when it eschews the creative process inherent in the cosmos and attempts to take control, forming the world into the image and likeness of a limited human ego. This kind of control refuses participation, withholds exchange, and rejects the vulnerable. Those who attempt to form their lives and societies on such control assume a kind of dominating power that wipes out all that does not fit the master plan. In extreme form we see the results of this control in such events as the Nazi plan of the master race and its methodology of extermination. But we do it in smaller ways, too. We exterminate parts of ourselves that are troubling because they do not fit our well-defined goals. We eliminate people and aspects of nature from our company because they make us nervous by their difference.

A true creation, a real coming to be, requires chaos, and we are afraid of chaos. But the Spirit of God breathes over the waters of chaos in the beginning, and out of that union of breath and chaos comes all that is. Breath over chaos begins everything that is good. If we associate madness with chaos, then the creative process is a Divine Madness, and the human power that would take control of that process to form creation to its own limited ends is sin. Such sin has led us to this day in which we, as a world, are willing to destroy the earth rather than let go of our limited perspective regarding what that earth should become, how people on the earth should think, what they should believe, and according to what principles they should govern themselves. Our attempts to form the world into our image has driven us mad; our madness deforms us and we reject whatever we cannot control. This is the sin of the world.

A client came to me recently in great pain over her "sensitivity." Her work in business seemed to require of her a steely eye, a witty brain capable of reducing others to powerless grovelers, a sharp tongue, and a soul incapable of feeling. "I want to be a bitch. Only the bitch-woman can get ahead—no, only the bitch-woman can even maintain herself in the business world. I want to not feel. I want to be capable of the verbal retort that will put others in their place and demonstrate my power."

Instead, she was a woman intensely aware of psychic danger when it presented itself in the clothes of a successful business partner; she sensed the power of a political move that could reduce her to a peon if she made a wrong step; she felt a strong need to protect not only herself from this danger but even the person in power. She worried about losing a job she hated. She worried because she could not conform to a situation that contained, for her, all the elements of destruction. She didn't really want to "be a bitch," she told me later; she only wanted to know how to formulate her self into words and actions that would allow her to maintain her integrity as a woman and, at the same time, not leave her vulnerable to abuse.

In my study I have a picture of Old Washee, Topui-Naachai, a Navajo medicine woman. She is said to have been 103 years old when the picture was taken in 1880, but she looks ageless and strong. She sits on a large rock surrounded by the tools of her craft: earthenware bowls, herbs, earth, trees, and sky. Her left hand is clenched into a fist, showing determination rather than violence, and her right hand holds a bowl on her lap. Her moccasined feet rest flat on the earth.

I often look at her, seeing in her a kind of icon—an elemental woman looking at me, asking me who I am and what I am willing to become by my commitments and my actions. It is plain to me that she knows who she is, what her relationship is to earth and to God, that in her is no pretense, no conformity to what is less than creation. And I wonder who took the picture and why. Was she an oddity, being so old and so unique in her tribe as to be given the shamanistic powers of a medicine woman? Did the photographer recognize her womanstrength, so daring and nonconforming to the popular culture?

Her eyes question: What are you willing to endure? To what and to whom will you bond yourself? How much of the truth have you the strength to speak? What will you relinquish? Are you willing to let your healing powers loose in the world? Are you willing to stare evil down? Are you willing to learn the skill of weaving up the tattered shreds of a deformed society? Are you willing to weave up the tattered shreds of yourself? Where are the holes in you through which the power of life slips out and is lost? Have you the determination to conserve? Have you the humility to be simple and of earth? Have you the heart to be your self?

A WomanChrist spirituality urges us to become who we are, both as individuals and as women. It urges a kind of madness in the eyes of the world, a kind of action that seems chaotic in the service of creation. It is the madness of the prophet—the Divine Fool, who is also protester, artist, and sometimes saint. It is a madness that seeks to reform what has been malformed and to transform what has been deformed. It is a madness of hope that acts as if that hope were a reality and, by daring to so act, transforms the hope into reality.

This prophetic madness and creative "folly" of WomanChrist spirituality claims and proclaims such hidden realities as the connectedness of all life and the evil of war and pollution, the equality in value of the sexes as well as the value of our masculine-feminine difference, care and respect for the vulnerable, mutual exchange among individuals and nations, primacy of the poor in distribution of the world's goods, the sacramentality of body and the inherent blessing of the sensual, the creative power of both pleasure and pain, the reunion of all we have made dualistic, the priesthood of women as well as of men—and all by a process that emphasizes the power of being rather than the power that controls by domination.

WomanChrist spirituality incarnates a new image for living. Imagination functions as its power source and compelling qual-

ity. The image rises within and draws us to live out its reality—
the image of peace, the image of compassion, the image of co-
operation. Prayer becomes the living out of the image given. It
is an extroverted prayer of creative imagination. It is a prayer
living out the Christ—for us, the WomanChrist. The images we
live out are as many and as individual as the women and men
who imagine, and they are collective as well. That out of which
we live, incarnating it in our personal lives as well as in our
world, is our prophecy—the manner in which the Holy speaks
and acts through us in the process of creative transformation of
the deformed world.

In that living out we often appear mad. We whirl with a chaos
that is dizzying. But as we whirl in the dance of the Divine Fool,
we coalesce from nebula to nexus, becoming a new constellation
of life—a mandala of the human community containing in its
center the image of a compassionate God.

CHAPTER 13

Searching for Wisdom

Within each of us, if we dare allow the awareness, gnaws an insatiable yearning. May I never be without this mysterious longing, prays the mystic, for it is my life; it is the house of my God. In the center of this yearning God kisses the soul with the kiss of wisdom.

> The soul is kissed by God
> in its innermost regions.
>
> With interior yearning,
> grace and blessing
> are bestowed.
>
> It is a yearning to take on God's
> gentle yoke,
> it is a yearning to give one's self
> to God's way.[1]

The yearning as expressed above by Hildegard of Bingen takes many forms; it is often experienced as darkness or incompleteness or even loss. It is always a terrible vulnerability, for we sense in it—even if darkly—the truth of T. S. Eliot's words that the condition of being "kissed by God" is one of "complete simplicity, costing not less than everything." Solomon's yearning led him to let go of everything he had acquired in his kingly position, through which letting go he experienced the Gift of All.

> I entreated, and the spirit of Wisdom came to me.
> I esteemed her more than sceptres and thrones;
> compared with her, I held riches as nothing.

I reckoned no priceless stone to be her peer,
for compared with her, all gold is a pinch of sand,
and beside her silver ranks as mud.
I loved her more than health or beauty,
preferred her to the light,
since her radiance never sleeps.
In her company all good things came to me,
at her hands riches not to be numbered.
All these I delighted in, since Wisdom brings them,
but as yet I did not know she was their mother.

(Wisdom 7:7–12 JB)

There is a vastness to the motherhood of Wisdom into which we are drawn and a vastness created within us out of which we are birthed and then birth our life's story and our life's work. This vastness that is Wisdom's womb is the space, the environment, the atmosphere of all our yearning and the dense, intense caldron of all being: our everyday creations of self and the arts proceeding from self, as well as the flinging forth of stars and galaxies in the always-expanding universe. Our every yearning is the yearning of the creation for greater being; our every yearning is the breath and the kiss of Wisdom in our souls. And we feel her in all that is incomplete, all that is chaotic, all that is not yet. We feel her as a great hunger. A friend of mine hears her as a scream as he is drawn into the vastness—the primal aliveness, the birth cry, the explosion of the original fireball, the breaking free of the self from the undifferentiated human mass. The tortured and triumphant cry of resurrected life tearing through the dank ground of death.

We yearn because nothing is enough. We yearn because so much remains to be created, and still it will not be enough. We yearn because we must increase a yearning that even in itself is not enough. Annie Dillard insists on clarity about the yearning and about its price:

The universe was not made in jest but in solemn incomprehensible earnest. By a power that is unfathomably secret, and holy, and fleet. There is nothing to be done about it, but ignore it, or see. And then you walk fearlessly, eating what you must, growing wherever you can, like the monk on the road who knows precisely how vulnerable he is, who takes no comfort among death-forgetting men, and who carries his vision of vastness and might around in his tunic like a live coal which neither burns nor warms him, but with which he will not part.[2]

"I entreated, and the spirit of Wisdom came to me," says the King. What is it that we ask in this entreaty? And who in us asks it? It is the King who asks. The King within us represents the powerful masculine facet of the self, the organizer, principle of order, center of extroverted power. But the psychic King is incomplete without the Queen, Sophia, the Lady Wisdom. Within each of us the King has his throne, his sceptre, his crown, his storehouse of precious gems, his counselors with their knowledge of the logical and technical, his warriors and generals, his builders of the kingdom. Let us make no mistake. The King lives within us, is a powerful part of us; but if we are to be creative, if we are to grow and be transformed and become ever more complete, the King within needs to cry out for the Lady Wisdom. Solomon, the scriptural image of the King, declares:

> In each generation she [Wisdom] passes into holy souls,
> she makes them friends of God and prophets;
> for God loves only the man who lives with Wisdom.

> (Wisdom 7:27 JB)

Only when Wisdom and the King are united in a holy marriage in the soul, or psyche, can the self be complete and experience the presence of the Holy One. Our yearning, then, is the masculine within us crying out for completion, for the feminine power, the vastness of the womb, the activity of creation. The masculine cries out in each of us as individuals, in the men we have taken to our hearts and with whom we have joined our lives, and in the masculinized Western culture in which we live.

Perhaps because of the predominant power of the masculine in the culture—in our history, in our religions, in our education, in our professions—we are always in danger of pursuing the masculine within us in order to develop that facet of self for the benefits we are told we will receive from it. But masculine energy pursued for itself, out of relationship with its feminine counterpart, is a false masculine. It is ungrounded and dangerous to us. When we have lost ourselves to masculine pursuits (in the home or in the professional or business world)—power and prestige, organization and administration, logic and rationality, competition and enlightenment, scholarly degrees, being in charge, keeping things separate—we do feel an initial surge of excitement. But the excitement is eventually followed by a numbing purposelessness and despair. We truly have "lost ourselves."

A businesswoman came to me for spiritual direction because she was feeling increasing ennui and diminishment of her desire to live. At work the pace was truly "type A," the emphasis was on perfection and quick decision making, the dealing with business associates was "tough" and objective without consideration of personal feelings. "I can only succeed here if I become hard and unfeeling," she said with cold anger in her eyes, "and I *will* succeed. I will beat these men at their own game and gain position in this company if it kills me!" And it was killing her. This woman was suffering from an interior divorce. In her pursuit of success she had mistakenly cut herself off from her own feminine energy and, consequently, from her creativity.

All of us have been tempted into this position at one time or another, whether at work in the professional or business world or at home with spouse and family. Masculine energy divorced from the feminine is so direct, so clear, so seemingly simple. We even have been tempted toward it in our spirituality, believing we can become disembodied spirits projected toward the Light of God. What can bring us to wholeness? How can we take up the search for Wisdom?

We need to encounter and submit to our yearning for what is beyond power, success, organization, and even enlightenment. Such yearning within calls us to an awareness of our need for Wisdom. And, paradoxically, this yearning proceeds from a masculine energy. It is the masculine yearning that constellates the vastness within which Wisdom will form a new creation. Anne Sexton writes of this process of being husbanded by the masculine and thereby brought to Wisdom. Note that at the beginning of the poem the woman is caught in an unbalanced masculine pursuit, and at the end she has been brought—still unsatisfied and somewhat enraged by what she has to let go—to Wisdom's nourishing womb.

THE GOD-MONGER

With all my questions,
all the nihilistic words in my head,

I went in search of an answer,
I went in search of the other world
which I reached by digging underground,
past the stones as solemn as preachers,
past the roots, throbbing like veins
and went in search of some animal of wisdom,
and went in search, it could be said,
of my husband (i.e. the one who carries you through).

Down.
Down.
Down.
There I found a mouse
with trees growing out of his belly.
He was all wise.
He was my husband.
Yet he was silent.

He did three things.
He extruded a gourd of water.
Then I hit him on the head,
gently, a hit more like a knock.
Then he extruded a gourd of beer.
I knocked once more
and finally a dish of gravy.
Those were my answers.
Water. Beer. Food.
I was not satisfied.

Though the mouse
had not licked by leprous skin
that was my final answer.

The soul was not cured,
it was as full as a clothes closet
of dresses that did not fit.
Water. Beer. Gravy.
It simply had to be enough.
Husband,
who am I to reject the naming of foods
in a time of famine?[3]

The quest for Wisdom is never a quest for answers. Rather, Wisdom resolves dualities into the mystery of paradox. Not from question to answer; rather, from question to questing. The quest for Wisdom is not from mystery to solution; rather, it is from mystery to greater Mystery. And it is a questing that goes *down*. The mystery of Wisdom is *in* creation; it is grounded in earth; it is contained in matter. To find her we must be willing to let go of pure spirit, of disembodiment, of hatred of the body, of disgust for the mess life often is. To find her we need to cease collecting answers to our lives—answers in our heads that no longer fit our lives, like clothes in our closets that no longer fit our bodies. The quest for Wisdom requires a descent into simplicity—a descent like the descent of Inanna into the underworld. She was required to divest herself. The descent was a letting go, an uncovering, a reduction to essence.

Wisdom only comes to us when we have been stripped of all that is ego-acquired so that we can depend on the most powerful energies of creation for our being and our identity. Wisdom appears only when we finally become aware that we are not God, that we are not required to be God, that we need not exercise a godlike control over our selves, our families, our worlds. Wisdom appears when we have become aware, through the stripping of descent, that we are one with creation and that she, Wisdom, is our life force. She is the energy by which we live. She is the center and the circumference. She is the subjectivity of all activity that does not diminish our being.

But if masculine energy has hold of us to the exclusion of the feminine, if we, like the poet, suffer from all the questions, all the nihilistic words in our heads and are always off in search of answers, where is the positive masculine energy that can constellate the vastness and call us toward Wisdom?

Masculine energy differs in men from the way in which it manifests itself in women. In men the mature masculine is introverted and ego-identified. The man can say, "I *am* masculine." The man whose masculine energies are mature has rooted those energies in the feminine ground of this self so that the energy he sends forth into the world is grounded. These are the really powerful men we sometimes experience who are neither macho nor ego-identified with the feminine. There can be no mistake about their masculinity: we feel the power of it projected through all they are and do. But such men are also and obviously connected by their souls to earth. Their strength is tender; their determination finds its basis in the essential realities of nature;

they are sensuous, in touch with and respectful of matter, of body, of earth; nature provides refreshment and renewal for their souls, and they hike and hunt and fish, climb mountains, and go on adventures to touch the Great Mother in her most primitive and primal places and to root their masculine energies more securely in her vast and inexhaustible power. These men are the husbands.

Masculine energy in a woman is extroverted. Through it we connect ourselves to world activities. But it is not, and cannot be, ego-identified. The ego is feminine, and that feminine ego must keep hold of the masculine energies while they are exercised in daily affairs or else the masculine will shoot off into the stratosphere of spirit like a missile that has lost contact with earth's mission control. And that extroverted masculine energy shooting out in straight linear power takes all our identity with it and leaves us exhausted and our lives meaningless—despite whatever power and success we may have achieved through that launching of the masculine.

So what can bring us back? When we have been torn apart at the core of self, what can reconnect us? We need, like Anne Sexton, to go in search of some animal of wisdom, to go in search, it could be said, of a husband (i.e., the one who carries you through).

The husband is the house-holder. Let me say here that not every man is, nor can he be, a husband. Only the man who truly holds the house within himself can be the husband—only the man who is an "animal of wisdom" can be the husband. The husband holds the house—the place of living, the space within which one is nourished and brought to life. He is the holder, the carrier, and the container of Wisdom. The husband is the masculine holder of the feminine. He is the one who carries us through.

When we have lost ourselves in masculine pursuits, we need to experience masculine questing. That questing is a threshold experience, a journey toward the doorway of the unknown home for which we have always longed. It is the masculine husband who carries us over the threshold. It is the marriage of the masculine with the feminine in us that brings us home to the self. When, finally, the feminine within us is husbanded, the King's

quest for the Lady Wisdom consummates in a marriage of opposites, a psychic intercourse by which the mature self is conceived and born.

At first we may not find husbanding a satisfying condition,
because we do not receive answers. Wisdom responds to our
quest with nourishment—water, beer, and gravy—rather than
with answers that do not satisfy because they very quickly do
not fit our questions.

"It simply had to be enough," the poet submits. Wisdom, the
life giver, answers our quest for meaning with food. "Husband,
who am I to reject the naming of foods in a time of famine?" It
is the Wisdom of all spirituality. It is manna. It is milk and
honey. It is water and salt. It is bread and wine. It is body and
blood. It is Eucharist. The quest for heaven is down, into earth,
into the womb of the Great Mother Sophia. The masculine energies in both men and women must be thrust into the womb of
the feminine Wisdom to be creative.

The way of God is the way of Wisdom. Our womanfaith
needs to be a response to Wisdom's call from where she dwells
in the depth of creation. The way of the masculine in our selves
is that of penetration of her depths. The faith of our masculine
energies penetrates earth and roots itself in her mystery. The
way of the feminine in our selves is identification with the
ground of creation's being and power. The faith of the feminine
is to be vastness—the live coal that neither burns nor warms but
with which we will not part. The faith of the feminine is to be
nourishment—the bread and wine, water, beer, and gravy—for
a famished humanity. The faith of the feminine is to become
ground, to become the depths, to accept embodiment and to love
bodiliness. The faith of the feminine is to be husbanded—carried
over the threshold to new life in the house of Wisdom.

CREATION'S WOMB

On a January day in California I drove down Reliez Valley
Road to Briones Park to walk in the hills. The sun angled its
light and warmth on the slopes, which were green and slippery
from the winter rains. I wore my Irish knit sweater—the tem-
perature was about sixty-five degrees. As I walked, the hills soon
closed around me in a sheltering, and I found myself completely

alone, with only an occasional airplane sound to remind me of our technological civilization. A Minnesota spring sound of running water called me to the edge of a small winding stream lined, where it ran through the hills, with mossy oak and gnarled chestnut trees. Birds joined their songs riotously, as if this were the first day of creation and they were trying out their newly found and extraordinary gift. I thought, "It is April."

A friend who knows the meaning of April to me had written some weeks before, "I have this totally untested theory that people who live in unwintered climates never experience spring quite like we do. You'll have to let me know whether there might be any validity at all in my theory. Who knows what spring from a snowless place might be like? Perhaps there is no April, or maybe it comes in February. . . ."

Now I think that April is probably a state of mind. I know that in the hills of Briones Park April came in January. It came as complex as it always comes. As T. S. Eliot reminds us:

> April is the cruelest month, breeding
> Lilacs out of the dead land, mixing
> Memory and desire, stirring
> Dull roots with spring rain.[4]

And e. e. cummings muses:

> —let the world say "his most wise music stole
> nothing from death"—
>   you only will create
> (who are so perfectly alive) my shame:
> lady through whose profound and fragile lips
> the sweet small clumsy feet of April came
> into the ragged meadow of my soul.[5]

April, I believe, is the absolutely new, the completely resurrected creation. April is the awareness that comes suddenly that I have been living a winter, my earth dry or frozen, my most wise words able to steal nothing from death. All at once memory and desire mix in the soul—the past and future transform in creation's alchemy to become my most alive present. And she who is most alive comes on her sweet small clumsy feet into the ragged meadow of my soul.

I felt how all that I have known of death—of those I love as well as of the death of heart that paralyzes hope and dries up memory at the same time as it strangles desire—I felt how all that I have known of death cannot hold me forever, because April comes again and again. The winters come and go. And the wisdom is in the ever-recurring April. The heart comes alive again in great shuddering spasms, and the whole body weeps tears that wash the world. The shuddering heart mixes memory and desire, stirring dull roots with spring rain.

In each coming of April, each stirring of life after death, each mixing of memory and desire, comes the certainty that we have been so visited before—a visit we cannot quite remember—and that this visit, for all of its present intensity, will fade into a similar forgetfulness. And we take in as much creation as we have life for and let it place its imprint on us—knowing it will transform us in a manner not dependent on memory.

Wisdom acts in creation as that which holds together and that which calls us to quest. She is both the being and the becoming of creation. She is the subjective consciousness, and everything else is the expression, the body. Wisdom is a caldron of paradox where chaos gives order, multiplicity integrates into unity, dark cannot be separated from light, nor life from death, body from soul, knowledge from experience.

The Fall we read about in the Genesis creation myth was, among other things, a way of talking about the loss of wisdom from the human psyche. Mythologically, there is only one tree— the axis of the world, the center pole, that which connects the levels of existence (what is below with what is above). But in the creation story we are presented with a division of this tree into two: the tree of life and the tree of the knowledge of good and evil—and we are commanded not to eat of the tree of knowledge. In his book, *Return of the Goddess* Edward Whitmont interprets this split to represent two modes of consciousness. In even more ancient myths the tree of life was rooted in an underground spring from which flowed life, enlightenment, and wisdom. Wisdom comes to us from life itself, from the direct experience of life, from sinking our roots into the unlimited flow of life. But to eat from the tree of knowledge separates knowledge from life. At least one meaning of the Original Sin is this dualism, this separation at the core of experience—the choosing of knowledge at the expense of wisdom.

This is the pride of believing that we can know without participating in the very creation itself. This is the arrogance we manifest when we set ourselves apart from creation as if we were its master and it simply an object for our use and manipulation. We are creation. We can know nothing real without drinking from the stream that flows from the tree of life. Wisdom flows as essence through our experience and calls us to drink—to participate.

When I was a young woman my dearest friend and mentor was fond of saying, "Years from now you will add my words to meanings." She knew of my heroic quest for knowledge—a more masculine- than feminine-originated energy that often develops in those women who enter professions early in life rather than marry early to devote their young years to the more feminine experience of mothering. The quest is masculine whether in a man or a woman. The challenge to set out on the quest and the being in which the quester is grounded is feminine. Eventually, we need to find the source, the ground at the roots of the tree of life, out of which comes the water of wisdom. We need to drink from the river of life, from the source of wisdom— and we need to come to that flowing feminine water consciously as the result of a masculine quest.

She, the feminine, is the Lady Wisdom through whose profound and fragile lips the sweet small clumsy feet of April came into the ragged meadows of my soul. It is she who mixes memory and desire, stirring dull roots with spring rain. It is she who requires our faith that the opposites within us can be held in a caldron of transformation until they are transformed into a meaningful unity.

A SPIRITUALITY OF WISDOM

Our spirituality is a mystery that cannot be told intellectually—analytically—with knowledge separated from life itself. Our spirituality joins earth and heaven, body and soul, past and future, human and divine in a circle of creative wisdom birthing all that is. We can try to speak it in fumbling words: poetry and story are best. We can dance it, make meals out of it, grow roses, parent children, ritualize in worship or social-political activism, make love, make joy, make play; we can cry it, shout it, build new societies out of it, heal the wounded through the wounds we have received in our embracing of it. We can recognize Wisdom in the simplicity and paradox of everything: an old woman's smile, a rainbow, a moth drawn to flame. We live each moment in a Wisdom of the Allness of God.

A friend writes, "I have become so convinced that the secret to living and being happy (and holy as well) is so very simple. It is acceptance. It is consent. The other day I was standing by my sink washing dishes and gazing at the hills when a realization seeped into me. Faith is different now. Formerly I spent a lot of time and derived a lot of pleasure and excitement from intellectual discovery, finding an organized system that more or less explained life. As I changed I simply reorganized or expanded the system of my beliefs. I had lots of questions, but I had lots of answers too.

"It seeped into me in my kitchen the other day that I don't have any of that anymore. I can *remember* all of it, but it doesn't matter. I don't have faith in it. Instead, faith has become a movement of being, a way of resting in Life itself. I cannot put words to it or organize it into a system so that I can understand it. I can't understand it. I'm not even always aware that I have it or do it or be it. It is a universal resting place—a call waiting for my absolute acceptance. Acceptance of *what is*. It isn't intellectual. I can't formulate exactly *what* is accepted. It just is.

"So I talk to myself: Be true. You are and will be cared for. Everything is God's embrace. Don't worry about anything that you are or have done or might be. You *are*. Embrace yourself as the Holy One embraces you—with everything: the messiness, the wonder, the impatience, the intensity, everything. You are so *beautiful*. So irreplaceable. So much a mystery. You are loved by God as if you alone were the only creation. And you are loved just as you are."

In my friend's experience masculine questing and feminine being unite in the simple and full acceptance of Life itself.

In Christianity the feminine Wisdom incarnates herself in the masculine Jesus. The masculine quester incorporates the feminine challenge to be and to become. The fullness of this unity— the resolution of questing and being—is the meaning of the Christ. "In Christ there is no male nor female"; rather, there is the marriage of masculine and feminine energy. Christ and Sophia are one. Christ incarnates Wisdom—the outpouring of the

Holy God—she who plays the creation, dances out being, births the cosmos in orgasmic pleasure of bringing forth. She it is also who is the source of suffering and chaos, darkness and mystery. She it is who requires that we contain the paradox of our existence bravely and by containment become a caldron for transformation. She is present in crucifixion as well as in resurrection.

She, Wisdom, is given to Job as response to and healing of his outrageous pain and loss: the Wisdom of God who "laid [earth's] cornerstone, when all the stars of the morning were singing with joy" (38:6 JB), "who pent up the sea behind closed doors, when it leapt tumultuous out of the womb" (38:8 JB), who has "journeyed all the way to the sources of the sea, [and] walked where the Abyss is deepest" (38:16 JB).

Job's pain is part of the pattern of creation, inherent in the process of cosmic becoming. The answer to his quest for meaning is Wisdom. "Do you really want to reverse my judgment?" says the Holy One from which creation flows. Do you want to "put me in the wrong to put yourself in the right"? (40:8 JB). The answer to all our lives is creation itself and the Divine Wisdom that forms it and is its process of becoming. Our spirituality needs to be one of becoming more and more sensitive to Wisdom and of living in accord with her. We are creation. We are the movement of Wisdom. Outside of her we are nothing, we cannot exist.

We discover Wisdom by attending creation. We are midwives in this birthing of the Holy, in this Divine Incarnation. In attending we learn empathy; we experience our connection with all being; each of us begins to feel the heartbeat of God in our bodies and the real oneness of our bodies with one another and with all material being. Wisdom makes our connection tangible. How, then, can we help but love what we are? And Wisdom is the love that communicates that we are the Body of God. Once we locate Wisdom in the center of Being, the limits of consciousness expand to include all, to love all. The center of my subjectivity can no longer be my own limited ego once I have let myself go to Wisdom; rather, I consciously become an expression of the subjectivity that is Wisdom herself. I become a fragment of her Incarnation. I become a member of the Body of Christ. I become WomanChrist.

The Apostle Paul was fond of calling Christ the "New Creation." This title insists on the cosmic dimensions of the Christ as well as Christ's inclusiveness of each individual fragment of creation. Christ as "New Creation" points to an identification of Christ with the process of becoming, for we are aware from the science of physics that all of being is constantly becoming, moving out, moving in, exploding, imploding, unfolding, forming, transforming, integrating, disintegrating, birthing, dying, rising.

Christ is the still point of this process as well as the turning twisting cosmic dance. Christ *is* the new creation. The energy or spirit of creation is Wisdom. And the creation and its energy are one. The two are one. Christ and Wisdom are one.

We find it extremely difficult to say just what Wisdom is. The literature of the Old Testament seems to indicate that Wisdom is the mystery of the order of creation—an order that creation can never reveal totally. That same literature personifies Wisdom as a woman, Sophia. But the vastness of her mystery continually defies that personification, just as all personifications of God are ultimately powerless to contain or to express the vastness of Ultimate Being. God remains the nameless One.

We seem filled with insatiable desire to find Wisdom. We engage constantly in the masculine quest. We sharpen our knowledge and skill to penetrate the farthest reaches of outer space and the unfathomable minuteness of subatomic space. And we perceive her subtle dance, the motion of her order, the manifestation of her presence, but we do not find Wisdom nor grasp her mystery, which both is the essence of creation and transcends it. Wisdom is the heart of God.

Wisdom is the Dance of being, the Mystery and order of creation, the Soul of the cosmos. She is the meaning, the Word. She is the "let it be." Wisdom that "comes forth from the mouth of God" echos continually through the ever-expanding universe. The book of Proverbs tells us that Wisdom was the first act of Yahweh, the initial generation of God's being.

> Yahweh created me when his purpose first unfolded,
>   before the oldest of his works.
> From everlasting I was firmly set,
>   from the beginning, before earth came into being.
> The deep was not, when I was born,
>   there were no springs to gush with water,

Before the mountains were settled,
　　before the hills, I came to birth;
before he made the earth, the countryside,
　　or the first grains of the world's dust,
When he fixed the heavens firm, I was there,
　　when he drew a ring on the surface of the deep,
when he thickened the clouds above,
　　when he fixed fast the springs of the deep,
when he assigned the sea its boundaries
　　—and the waters will not invade the shore—
　　when he laid down the foundations of the earth,
I was by his side, a master craftsman,
　　delighting him day after day,
　　ever at play in his presence,
at play everywhere in his world,
　　delighting to be with the [children of humankind].

(Prov. 8:22:31 JB)

There is no small argument among scripture scholars regarding this image of Wisdom. Most of them seem intent on differentiating the Hebrew image of Wisdom from the personified goddesses of Wisdom in surrounding cultures, for example, from the Egyptian goddess Maat. Translated simply, her name is "Mother." She is original, the Mother of God. Paradoxically, she is also the world-creating daughter of a father god. She establishes justice in the universe—the order of wisdom.

The feminine consciousness prefers less differentiation, finding delight in the possibility of such intermingling of divine imagery between cultures. The complexity of many divine images provides depth to understanding and belief. Personification grounds that belief, gives it a bodysoul. It is not so much that different cultures believe in a different God; it is that we experience the Ultimate Mystery we call God presented to us in a variety of images. Wisdom is Maat in Egypt, Minerva in Rome, Tiamat in Babylonia, Mat Hatti in Northern Syria, Matu in the African Pygmy culture, Sophia in Greece, Shekina to the Jew, Christ to the Christian. Each image provides a facet through which to experience this Mystery.

But is there anything that distinguishes Judeo-Christian Wisdom from the others? In his extensive study, *Wisdom in Israel*, Gerhard Von Rad concludes that Sophia, Shekina, Wisdom in our

Scriptures, *calls.* This is her distinction. She loves humankind and beckons us from within and without to participate in her dance—the dance of creation.

Her call is ultimately the same as the command of Yahweh. "I have set before you life and death. . . .Choose life" (Deuteronomy 30:19 JB).

The choice between life and death is also a choice for love—love of creation, love of the dance of Divine Wisdom. Love of her is love of life itself. Neglect of Wisdom brings world destruction. She is the Mother, the womb of all, the movement of birth, the great circle of being. She is powerfully accessible in our yearning for greater life and deeper understanding.

> Wisdom is bright, and does not grow dim.
> By those who love her she is readily seen,
> and found by those who look for her.
> Quick to anticipate those who desire her, she makes
> herself known to them.
> Watch for her early and you will have no trouble;
> you will find her sitting at your gates.
> Even to think about her is understanding full grown;
> be on the alert for her and anxiety will quickly
> leave you.
> She herself walks about looking for those who are worthy
> of her
> and graciously shows herself to them as they go,
> in every thought of theirs coming to meet them.
>
> (Wisdom 6:12–16 JB)

It is not only we who seek; this fundamental Mystery of creation comes seeking us. It is not only we who yearn; the Divine Wisdom yearns for us as well. She yearns for us so intensely as to become one of us, incarnated specifically in the creation as a human person—Jesus, the Christ. She who comes forth from the mouth of God, the Word in whom all things were made, became flesh and dwelt among us.

Our faith, our spirituality, then, is the living out, in the common experiences of every day, of the yearning of Wisdom for greater being. She yearns in us and calls us to quest. She is our yearning and the energy of our quest. She is the ground of being into which we descend looking for some "animal of Wisdom."

She it is who is our Mother and the Womb from which we are born. We come forth from her each moment wet with the birthing waters of a more whole being.

CHAPTER 14

Finding Wisdom in Ourselves

Although we can personify Wisdom in various images and, for the purposes of clarity and simplicity, discuss these images separately, Wisdom in her essential creative energy is really the synthesis of images. She is present wherever there is in our creation a reconciliation of opposites. Wisdom is active whenever what is below is drawn together with what is above, when the shadow is united with the image of light. When the dualities we have constructed to make our task of identification and power taking easier are returned to their original wholeness, we know that the spirit of Wisdom is present.

In Christian tradition an ancient image for Mary is the Seat of Wisdom. As such she is both the ground for the incarnated Wisdom and his feminine prototype. Mary is the original WomanChrist. She can provide for us a model of reconciliation of opposites that we experience every day in our lives as women. In her life Mary lived out Wisdom as cosmic weaver, who gathers together the multicolored threads of creation and from the chaos weaves a pattern of universal meaning. Such is the weaving that takes place in each of our individual lives by entwining the seemingly chaotic threads of our experience. One could imagine Mary the young girl, or any of us women at any time in our lives, praying to Wisdom, the Weaver, that the inexplicable and often opposite threads of our lives might form a pattern of beauty:

> Weaver, your threads are wild
> With winds of tomorrow;
> Wind my life into your tapestry,
> Take the lore of all my days

And, with the varied hues
Of lakes, of forests, mountains, and the sea,
Weave my story through the pattern of your web.

Take the woodland pathways
From my childhood days,
The wildflower meadows leading to vast waters,
Secluded coves where gulls soared,
Tangled driftwood beaches,
Ancient rock islands holding fast against time,
And the relentless lake.
Take the solitude
Of an only child
Watching the night sky
For the first star.
And weave me, Weaver, into the pattern of your web.

Take the youthful dreamer
Spinning images of endlessness
In the aching beauty of sunsets
And the wonder of a rising dawn.
Take the pristine ecstasy
Of first love,
Every touch and tear and kiss,
Every bittersweet meeting and goodbye,
And weave me, Weaver, into the pattern of your web.

Take the pathways of the mind
That I have walked in search of truth;
Take my midnight dance at the dark of the moon;
Take the veil and the ancient song of holiness;
Take my silence in the wheatfields
Every fruitful summer afternoon;
Take the voices of my children
Whispering the stories of their might-have-been lives;
Take the closing in of winter, every year;
Take the roses that have never died;
And weave me, Weaver, into the pattern of your web.

Four essential and opposite images contained in the feminine
and needing to be woven together by the power of Wisdom are
the virgin and the mother, the bride and the widow. I would
like to explore with you the meaning of each of these images
separately, as well as the pattern of the feminine web they make
when reconciled with each other.

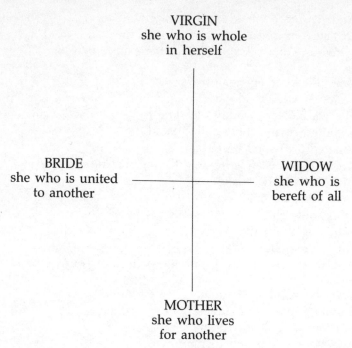

VIRGIN
she who is whole
in herself

BRIDE
she who is united
to another

WIDOW
she who is
bereft of all

MOTHER
she who lives
for another

POWER OF CREATION

WISDOM THE VIRGIN

When I was a child in the Roman Catholic church, the ideal of virginity attracted me. Sister in her black robe and veil concealed something mysterious that was more than physical, and I wanted to know what it was. Stories of women saints almost always included a scene in which the young girl, rebellious with holiness, defied her rich father's desire that she marry an equally rich king or nobleman, declaring that she would be the bride of God alone. Some of these willful girls went to great lengths to emphasize their decision and make themselves "unmarriageable." I thrilled to tales of young women running away from home, chopping off their beautiful hair, or hiding away in attic rooms. My fascination began long before I understood that sex and virginity had anything to do with each other. These were young women who intended to live life as they saw it, regardless of parental injunctions or cultural norms. They touched the impulse toward the heroic within me and tantalized the imagination of this "good Catholic child" with the notion of holy rebellion. Early on I determined to join their small and mysterious society—a society of virgins.

Of course, I knew this would mean no marriage and no family, and that seemed reasonable. Marriage appeared quite conventional to my young romantic heart and unable to stimulate the heroic and individualistic gift of soul required of the woman who stood alone. Nor did aloneness seem to require a distaste for or distance from men. Clare had her Francis, after all. I fell in love early and intensely. It was no secret from family, friends, and the small town community in which I lived. In fact, I felt somewhat compelled to demonstrate that this love and my choice of a virginal life did not contradict one another.

The paradox I lived at that young age was at the level of archetype rather than reason. I would have staked my life on the certainty that I could be both virgin and lover. And I have never changed my mind about that. At seventeen years of age I promised union of soul eternally and assured the young man that we would meet in heaven. I carried the love for him in my heart as I went off to the convent to give myself, undivided, to God.

She who is virgin is the woman who is one or whole in herself. Each woman contains this image or archetype, either in her active life or in the shadow of her soul. Phases of life, if not her entire life, are influenced by virgin power, and that virginal energy can become for any women a reservoir of special wisdom. We do not, contrary to general opinion, cease to be a virgin when we become sexually active, for sex is but a symbol (a magnificent one) for what transpires in the soul. If in the sexual embrace I cease to be whole in myself, I do, for that period of time, lose my virginity by giving psychic ascendency to a different image—perhaps that of the bride. But the virgin remains alive within and can be recovered intact.

We are not accustomed to thinking this way. We so identify virginity with physical sexuality that we think of ourselves as having irretrievably "lost our virginity" with our first sexual encounter. We are then, forever after, not a virgin. This is an unfortunate misappropriation of a word; it is reductionistic and sorely limits a complex and ancient image. The virgin goddesses of mythology were almost never without sexual encounters. Vestal virgins, in the service of the goddess Vesta (Hestia), although they lived in a society of women in the service of the gods, received men—particularly warriors—in their sexual embrace to purify them of war or other intense masculine pursuits by grounding them again in the feminine. Sex in this context had the sacred purpose of purification and union with the holy and in no way affected the virginity (oneness in herself) of the vestal virgin.

In Christianity Mary, the Virgin-Mother of Jesus, has also suffered from reductionism. As a consequence we have engaged in strange speculations about how Mary remained physically intact throughout the conception and birth of her son. Many of us have a mystical image of conception by breath and birth in a shaft of light, both events involving Mary's body little or not at all.

Instead of literalizing, we could have been wondering all these years about the mystery of one woman becoming, in a single image, the representation of archetypal opposites—the virgin and the mother. Mary is she who simultaneously is one in herself and lives for her child. In all of mythology no goddess represents this combined archetype. Each goddess is a virgin or a mother or represents a transition from the one to the other. But Mary is the virgin who is also, at the same time, the mother, and she is the mother who remains totally the virgin. Any woman who has attempted to live out these opposites in her own life will recognize here a profound mystery, one far deeper and more relevant for our living than how a woman might conceive without benefit of male penetration. Surely, by reducing this mystery to the physical we have deprived ourselves of an archetypal image that could provide the modern woman with a wealth of energy to engage in the tasks set before us by these times. We have within us the power to be virgin-mother, to reconcile the opposites of feminine energy into a transformed way of being and acting in the world.

Before opposites can be reconciled, however, they need to be differentiated. We need to distinguish characteristic energies of the virgin and the mother and of the bride and the widow. Only after so clarifying the opposites can we grasp the significance of the power they release when they form their paradoxical conjunction in the human psyche: the virgin-mother and the widow-bride. The goal here is a differentiated integration.

Wisdom as virgin finds her most characteristic image in the

Greek goddess Athene. Athene, after whom the great city of Athens was named, has been called the original daughter of the fathers because of her birth, fully formed and armored, from the head of her father, Zeus. That she was originally conceived within the goddess, Metis ("Female Wisdom"), whose pregnant body was swallowed by Zeus, is often ignored by those who relate the story of her birth. Athene is born of the father only because he first incorporated into himself the wisdom of the feminine.

Some authors downplay Athene's "birth" from the father to emphasize her parthenogenic conception. In Egypt the goddess Isis was sometimes called Isis Athene, which meant, "I have come from myself." She and Metis combine into one image—the original feminine creative energy, the ground of Wisdom.

In the virgin, Athene, wisdom is practical. She is the maker, the worker, the creator of cities and nations. She whispers her inspiration to the general, her courage and strategy to the warrior, her sense of order to the poet. She is the soul maker who inserts Psyche, the butterfly, into the bodies of newly created human beings.

Athene's virginity is not lonely, for she is friend to man and woman equally. But as virgin, her friendship is free of entanglement, her boundaries are clearly defined, and her sense of self is sharp and pure.

When we as Christians look to Mary as virgin, we are doing a revolutionary thing. In Hebrew tradition it was not acceptable for a woman to be "virgin." Her soul and body were to be at the service of the nation seeking to produce a Messiah. But the event of the Christ needed virginal space as well as a mothering ground—a fullness of feminine wisdom. The Christ needed not simply a mother but a virgin-mother.

So Mary was a re-volution. She was a rolling back—a *volutare*. In her the feminine revolved and reincorporated images from the past. One facet of Mary's being is the wisdom of the virgin, much as this wisdom is imaged in Athene. This is not to say that Mary was historically influenced by Greek mythological thought. Rather, it is to say that as a Christian prototype Mary contains the same virginal archetype that formed the psychic content for the Greek image of Athene.

We call Mary the Seat of Wisdom, the Mirror of Justice, and the Tower of Ivory. These "titles" have, no doubt been interpreted in many ways throughout the centuries, but as poetic descriptions they continue to provide us with unlimited reflection and insight. As virgin, Mary is the Seat of Wisdom: the ground, the feminine underpinnings on which wisdom rests and out of which it proceeds. For the word *seat* not only means a kind of "chair" on which one sits; it also can indicate the source or center out of which something arises, as, for example, "The mind is the *seat* of intelligence." The Christ, incarnated Sophia or Wisdom, not only rests on Mary as in the ancient frescoes of Mary forming a kind of chair for the child, Jesus; he also proceeds from her, is born from her, comes out of her. She is the Seat of Wisdom.

She is the Mirror of Justice. The wisdom of the virgin provides an ordering energy within creation. Justice, that order of life and experience that we find when a deep love for being exists, is mirrored in Mary. In other words, Mary both reflects creation at its best and is a mirror for each of us. When we look at her, our personal image is reflected off of her prototypical image. Seen in and through her eyes, we discover the virginal one-in-selfness that gives order to our own souls. It is out of that wholeness and order that we can find the authenticity to act justly in the world, thus furthering the creative process.

She is the Tower of Ivory. In this image Mary and Athene are connected in their armored aspect. Virginal wisdom manifests strong boundaries and limits, a decisive sense of where "I" end and another person begins. Athene's armor was decorated with the image of the Medusa, the feminine destroyer whose glance could turn to stone any who looked upon her unbidden. Virgin-wisdom does not allow penetration by another to diffuse the one-in-selfness. As Tower of Ivory, Mary portrays power in her self. She stands tall and contained. Her boundary is not harshly reflective armor but, rather, glowing ivory. Nevertheless, as a boundary the ivory is firm. The one who looks upon the Tower of Ivory is never turned to stone but rather from stone. Ivory itself is a living and receptive firmness that encourages us to shed our harsh armor for boundaries that are life-giving so that we will not fear to submit to the God whose promise is to take from us our stony hearts and give us hearts of flesh. Mary as Tower of Ivory loves and receives us without losing wholeness in her self.

The wisdom of the virgin differs from the wisdom of the mother in numerous ways that we need to consider before we can understand the virgin-mother archetype. In the reconciliation of opposites we have, as I have said before, a differentiated integration.

VIRGIN	MOTHER
Focused consciousness	Diffuse awareness
Goal direction	Process orientation
Self-motivation	Motivated by other's needs
Purposeful energy	Productive energy
Lives for the vision	Lives for the child
Values ideas	Values people
Emphasizes thinking	Emphasizes feeling
Order	Chaos
Realm of sky	Realm of earth
Future-oriented	Past-oriented
(finds future in present)	(finds past in present)
Chronological time (linear)	Cyclical time (spiral)
Relates to equals	Relates to the needy

The opposites we see here are never dissolved into one another within the soul but, rather, operate in a distinct simultaneity. The virgin and mother energies of wisdom are not contradictory; instead, they complete one another. Both are needed for creation.

WISDOM THE MOTHER

The mother image is extremely complex. Her frequent appearance in our dreams, in both her creative and her destructive aspects, attests to her power in our souls. She is the personified earth from which we are born and into which we die. She is the round, productive womb; the deep, consuming void; the overwhelming protector; the one who feeds us at and suffocates us against her breast. When we attempt to gain freedom from her, she searches us out, even to the depths of hell if necessary. She it is who can nourish, overnourish, or withhold food—material, spiritual, psychological.

The powerful mother energy has been more lauded and more

blamed, more idealized and more feared than, perhaps, any other. We first experience mother energy from our own real mothers and then, later, project on those same fragile human beings all of the numinous power of the mother archetype within our own psyches. We need goddesses to represent for us the Mother's extraordinary intensity for our own sakes and that of our mothers and children.

Mother wisdom proceeds from the eternal return, the spiral of life we experience in the seasonal turnings and returnings of nature and its seasons. This is a wisdom open to taking in, increasing, and producing everything. Here is the chaos of primal creation, that whirling potential inherent in what we call prime matter (primal mother). This is an energy that simultaneously excites and terrifies.

Some years ago, when I was being initiated into a greater awareness of mother energy in myself, I had a dream that was both simple and frightening. In my house I discovered an opening I had not noticed before. It was vulva-shaped and probably deep. I went closer to inspect it and its contents and discovered, to my terror, that a queen bee swollen with larvae sat in its womblike center. Out of herself she squeezed one larva after another, and I was immediately conscious that there would never be an end to this production. I awoke profoundly disturbed by the encounter.

We can be overwhelmed by the possibilities we contain, and such dreams can be a warning. This dream came to me at a time when I was entering into a strongly productive time of my life. Each day I found some new possibility for creative endeavor and felt it nearly impossible to say no to anyone or any project. My energy and excitement were higher than ever before. But I was blinding myself to the dangers that can result when any energy is carried too far. I needed some of the purposeful, goal-directed, orderly planning of a corresponding virginal energy to coexist with the powerful mother energy I was experiencing. I needed a reconciliation of opposites to assure meaningful creativity.

When we return to the source, the beginning of mother energy, we arrive, inevitably, at earth itself—Gaia. The wisdom of the Mother is, first of all, the wisdom of earth. She is prepersonal, pretemporal (she exists as one of the original deities before Chronos—Time—came to be). When the author of Genesis writes, "In the Beginning God created heaven and earth. Now the earth was a formless void, there was darkness over the deep" (1:1-2 JB), it is of Gaia he speaks. From her, then, comes all that is. She receives the impregnating Word and begins to give forth. She is the depth. She is the void, the chaos, the womb. She is the mother of mothers.

We long for her. We seek her complete giving and total receptivity in our own mothers and find only faint echoes of what we desire, for what we desire is divine. Our own mothers seek it as well. We feel vibrations of her birthing in our own bringing forth, but we can never bring forth enough to satisfy our longing for creation, because her urging within us is also divine. We may wander from her, but she always calls us back. When all abstractions are stripped away, when we have reached the limits of our intuition and our thinking to cast the light of meaning on our lives, we are left with Gaia. Then we kneel upon the earth, bend, feel the cool of her body on our foreheads and our hands, let the energy rise from her depths and invade us. We receive our power from her and release it into her again when we have been refreshed, healed, reborn. It is Gaia who mixes memory and desire—through whose profound and fragile lips the sweet small clumsy feet of April come into the ragged meadows of our souls.

We pray, usually without words:

> Holy Mystery of life,
> Mother in and of earth,
> Loving Nourisher of all being,
> Let me be, today, your body.
> Open my ears and my soul
> To listen and to hear:
> > The laughter and the pain,
> > The whispers and cries,
> > The silent pleadings in eyes looking at me.
> Be in my every response
> As Wisdom.
> For you are the Holy One
> Forever giving birth to all that is human,
> And I am your daughter.

This summer I spent a few days on the north shore of Lake Superior. The power of Gaia subsists there more than in most places of the world. Ancient stone, wooded cliffs, sheer drops of rock into the deep and turbulent lake all attest to her presence. We have not tried to tame her there, so her power oozes from the ground, crashes onto the rocks, and cries out from the dark forests.

With someone I had loved all my life I climbed through a birch forest to White Rock, from which we could view the vastness of forest and water. There we stood in silence for a long time. I felt within me first an immeasurable void left by the death of my spouse only two months before, then the slow power of life rising up from the rock, from the earth's depth. Deep called unto deep. Love for life, fullness of being, invaded me, impregnated me. I was in love. I lost my sense of objectivity from the earth. I *was* earth. Time ceased. Only the overwhelming energy of bringing forth remained. I felt on the verge of giving birth. I wanted only to give birth forever. I looked at my dear friend and found no separation there either. There was one power, one life, one being, and she was Gaia. I had nearly lost myself in death, and she restored, in a rebirthing that was both hers and mine simultaneously, the connections between my body and my soul.

When we come home again to earth in such a manner as to find there both the power of being itself and the soul of our own individual being, we have come into the wisdom of Gaia, the primal mother. She is the essence of being, the energy of creation. Earth and body are her manifestations. She is birthing power.

Although Wisdom in Gaia is primordial, she seeks personification. In Greek mythology the mother goddesses became increasingly more distinct as time passed in order to emphasize specific dimensions of motherhood, such as life given for the child and the fundamental experience of loss that we see in Demeter. In Christianity we look to Mary for such personification and specificity.

Although the tradition has been, again, reductionistic with regard to her, if we allow ourselves to strip the sentimentality from her image we can find in Mary the primal power of Gaia. In the beginning of the Gospel of St. John we find a reworking of the Genesis myth. We find there all the elements as in the first story of creation, but here the Word or seed of the Holy One comes "down from heaven" to penetrate the earth, which is the virgin, Mary. She is presented to us as primal matter, the mother of God. In her vast chaotic ground the Word becomes flesh.

The Church, then, appropriates to Mary much of the Wisdom literature; what is spoken of Wisdom—she who is the energy and body of creation, she who is the process of coming to be— is now spoken of Mary the Mother of God. "From eternity, in the beginning, he created me, and for eternity I shall remain" (Eccles. 24:9 JB). "I am the Mother of fair love, and fear, and wisdom and of holy hope."[1] . . . "Approach me, you who desire me, and take your fill of my fruits, for memories of me are sweeter than honey, inheriting me is sweeter than the honeycomb. They who eat me will hunger for more, they who drink me will thirst for more" (Eccles. 24:19–22 JB). We are reminded here of the river that flows from the roots of the tree of Life, the Mysterious Feminine, the source of Wisdom.

Mary, the Mother, is called House of Gold. She is the original house—the earth, the cosmic womb. She is the house of the Christ, the firstborn of all creatures, the fulfillment of creation. Within Mary as Gaia, creation undergoes the most miraculous of alchemies; it becomes "gold." Symbolically, gold and light are synonymous. Gold is to the earth as the heart is to a person. It is the center, the hidden treasure, the highest quality of transformation. She whose motherhood transforms ordinary matter into gold calls us to her house. In fact, we are at one and the same time called to become a part of the new creation she encloses and to join her by our own motherhood in the enclosing. Our mother wisdom is a house of the new creation. We are gold makers, Christ bearers.

She is the Ark of the Covenant. In Mary's mother wisdom the opposites are reconciled. The Covenant is the supreme uniting: that of the Divine with the human. She is the Mother within whose body earth and heaven are made one. She is the prototype of our motherhood: that ark of earth we carry with us throughout all our journey in life. Womanwisdom makes an ark of things of earth—wood and bone; purple, red, violet, and crimson linen; gold and silver—flesh of the Mother, knowing all the while she will carry lightning in her fragile frame. And the fire of the Covenant will fuse whatever has been separated by our denial, by our fear, or by our arrogance. Born from this mothering, we will become whole: human with divine, body with soul, spirit with flesh, masculine with feminine, virgin with mother.

POWER OF TRANSFORMATION

Wisdom reconciles opposites. In the images of the virgin and the mother this reconciliation happens in the activity of creation. So the spirituality that arises out of these feminine images is one of an extroverted creation spirituality. Creation, its process and activity, centers and unifies the opposites of virgin and mother. Both energies are necessary; both must keep their distinctness; neither can be dissolved into the other. We must be able to draw on the power of both, often simultaneously, in order to further the creative process.

The opposites of bride and widow are reconciled in the process of transformation. This is an introverted process of mysticism and contemplation. Finally, all four images join in a wholeness that includes both transformation and creation, introversion and extroversion, self and the world. But, again, to appreciate the integration it is first necessary to differentiate the images.

WISDOM THE BRIDE

In the bride the masculine and feminine energies are united in a dramatic transformation of the inner self. The relationship between the woman and the man becomes a sublime and embodied container for this transformation, which seems—through the union of two human persons—to be both personal and cosmic. Thus, the bride often thinks of her beloved and feels toward her beloved in images that include all of nature. A bride might express herself toward her human lover in a manner that includes everything in the transformation she is experiencing: her self, their union, and the transformation of all creation.

She might say: "Earth is our body, and we are never apart, never separate, never alone—we are one. This is the promise of creation in which we have participated, to which we have consented now so many times as we have looked into one another's eyes, as we have held one another, as we have shared ecstasy in a transformation of love. You are the multicolored autumn, the blue sky behind the golden aspen and flaming maple. It is you who moves my soul to sing and rejoice each moment, each breath I take. Your voice echoes through my life; your eyes shine everywhere I look; you touch me in the soft breeze and flow through me like sunlight. I love you gently, wildly, carefully, with abandon, honestly, recklessly, faithfully, passionately, with whispers and cries and laughter. I love you waking and sleeping, in excitement and in calm. I love you in the ordinary and in the magical. I love you making omelets, walking in the door after work, driving the car, reading the paper, watching T.V., ordering a meal, absorbing the moon on the water, leaning against the rock, dreaming in front of the fire, listening to music, holding me, searching my eyes, melding our beings. I pledge myself to you in truth and in fidelity forever. I give you my soul as a resting place to be a home for your heart and a healing for your mind. I give myself to you for union, for the fulfilling of our destiny. All the stars cry out with joy. The entire universe sings!"

Aphrodite's archetype has hold of the bride. She is the form of love, the one who springs fully formed from the foam of the sea. She does not grow gradually but, rather, appears suddenly in her full form and fills the soul with ecstasy.

The masculine lover bending toward the bride in undisguised yearning, the irresistible energy in the lover and the bride, forms a complex image. Both energies yearning for union are within the woman herself. They are also cosmic energies yearning for the transformation and completion of the entire universe. They find embodiment in a real man and woman, but not only there. The feminine energy in one woman may yearn for union with the masculine energy in another. Or, finally, the feminine or masculine energy in a woman may yearn for union with the masculine or feminine power in God.

Dreams and visions of women and men through the centuries and from a variety of spiritual traditions present the soul as bride of a powerful and loving divinity who ravishes with beyond-human penetration of sweetness and light and through this divine intercourse transforms the human soul. The Greek rites of Dionysus initiated women into masculine power, requiring them to uncover it within themselves, feel its wild ecstasy as they became maenads, suffer from their own desire for its intensity, feel themselves completed—holding the swooning god in their arms—and, finally, return to their daily lives transformed by the reconciliation of opposites. Christian saints, both men and women, experienced themselves as bride to a divine Lover. Teresa of Avila fainted with ecstasy in the divine embrace; John of the Cross composed erotic poetry to the Bridegroom of his soul; Therese of Lisieux offered her life as an oblation to the love of God. For hundreds of years women dedicating themselves to lives of prayer and love in religious communities heard themselves called on their day of profession: *"Veni sponsa Christi"*— "Come, bride of Christ."

The bride is, then, that facet of psychic feminine energy that transforms the self through the integration of the masculine— the masculine as human bridegroom, interior masculine power, cosmic masculine energy, or divine Bridegroom. For most of us these different forms of the masculine will be intertwined. In the love we feel for our spouse, for example, we will also experience an interior integration, the power of nature, and the presence of God. For some of us, or at particular times in our lives, a focus will be placed on a specific kind of integration. The celibate nun focuses on the divine Bridegroom and the integration of the human feminine soul with the divine masculine Spirit. The professional woman coming into her power in the world of work may experience the integration of the masculine through facets of herself she needs to develop in order to succeed in that work. The woman "in love" and preparing to commit herself to another person in marriage experiences transformation through that relationship. Any of these specific transformations are as a result of the ascendancy of the bridal image in the psyche.

The bride will do anything to be with her beloved. She will, like the scriptural one who is called, leave father and mother, house and lands and children. The power of this archetype to attract a person toward union of the fundamental energies in the universe and in the psyche is so strong as to make the person under its influence seem almost crazy by conventional standards. People literally change their style of life, their profession, their place of residence. They move to other lands. They become missionaries or Peace Corps workers. The successful lawyer leaves her comfortable home in the suburbs, buys a large house in the inner city, and opens a shelter for the homeless. The sedate doctor's wife and mother of eight falls in love with the world itself and joins a circle of women protesting war. Her life, her soul, her world are transformed by love as she stands in court defending her principles of justice. If it weren't for the intense bridal energy, such radical transformations couldn't even be considered.

But how do we recognize this energy within ourselves? What characterizes the image of the bride within? First of all, hers is a playful energy. It is an energy of being that becomes involved with life for its own sake and finds joy in that involvement. It is not directed toward a goal so much as it rejoices in the experience of ecstasy that a union of opposites releases. The bride possesses a synthetic attention to life. She attends. She stands before and receives. Within her all that is received is synthesized.

Bridal energy is intuitive. The bride's knowing is of the depths; like a stone dropped into a well, her understanding descends immediately and radically to life's source. She experiences transformation by fire. It is as if her soul were, in Annie Dillard's powerful image in *Holy the Firm*, a moth caught on the wick of a candle, becoming that wick, becoming light. She rejoices in this alchemy and barely feels the pain because of the intensity of light. She lives for the beloved, relating to him in everything—her self, nature, the human, and the divine. Her whole power of being is oriented toward eternity in that she discovers the eternal in each moment. Time for the bride is synchronistic—a meaningful coincidence of events that are not causally related but that give direction and purpose to her life.

In our Christian heritage Mary becomes the prototype of Wisdom as bride. We call her Morning Star, Cause of our Joy, and Gate of Heaven. As Morning Star, Mary recalls the goddess Aphrodite or Venus, who is also the morning star and the eternal bride. She is the form of love. She attracts the brilliant sun to transform darkness into daylight. Actually a planet rather than a star, the "Morning Star" is bathed in the transforming fire of the sun and shines because of the integration of opposites—the ground of the planet and the fire of the sun.

Mary is Cause of our Joy. In the Incarnation she was the bride who reconciled the opposites of human and divine, masculine and feminine, in her own bodysoul. In her we discover that such a transformation is possible for us as well. We are not limited to dualisms. We can be made whole; the earth can be made whole. It is the wisdom of the bride. God is present in all things, and all things are present in God. Our deepest consciousness is God-consciousness; our deepest subjectivity is divine. In Mary the Divine held intercourse with the human to transform both in the Christ. In Mary the masculine Word held intercourse with the feminine Sophia and was transformed into WomanChrist. Such transformation is the ultimate source of our Joy. The Cause of our Joy.

Finally, Mary is the Gate of Heaven. As Bride she opens herself to the Holy and becomes a gate by which we, too, might enter the Source and Fulfillment of Being. As Bridal Gate she is prototype of the cosmic feminine womb where all transformation of seed into full-blown life takes place. Her womb is the heaven in earth into which the Word as seed enters to be transformed by the alchemy of the flesh. She embodies the Word.

WISDOM THE WIDOW

Bridal power and wisdom balance in a paradox with the wisdom and power of the widow.

BRIDE	WIDOW
Synthetic attention	Detached concentration
Integration of opposites to form self	Disintegration of identity toward integrity of being
Motivated by attraction	Motivated by absence
Playful energy	Contemplative energy
Lives for the beloved	Lives for the cosmos
Values union	Values separation
Emphasizes intuition	Emphasizes sensation
Ecstasy	Grief
Realm of sea	Realm of the underworld
Eternity-oriented (finds eternal in present)	Present-oriented (finds present in eternal)
Synchronistic time	Timelessness—no time
Relates to opposites	Relates to the whole

The wisdom of the widow recognizes the inevitability of loss and its sacred quality. She is the woman at the center of the earth, the feminine power of the underworld. She is one of the untouchables because of the sacred power surrounding her. She has been to the boundaries of life where death sings her dark song. The widow has caught the melody, and its vibrations emanate from her, affecting anyone who comes close. She is a fearsome image within us, because we fear to lose any part of life, particularly that which we love.

The widow has lost her "husband"—the one who carries her through. The husband is that aspect of the masculine that transports us, that takes us through the door, that carries us over the threshold. The husband makes time possible, movement of life. Without this aspect of the masculine the feminine is stuck on the threshold itself. The woman becomes a liminal (threshold) person, neither in nor out. For her there is only an eternal present moment neither in nor out of time. Her existence is timelessness. Her home is to have no home. "It doesn't matter where I am," a recently widowed woman told me. "What I am—the one who has lost—is where I live, and it is everywhere I am."

The widow has descended into the underworld, beneath the surface of things. Her perspective on everything changes. She sees the world from the inside, from where the roots of all things grow. She is a root woman, a radical woman, a woman at the center—returned to the original space, the world-womb, the dark body of Wisdom. She is enclosed in the darkness of night, the thick darkness of blood. She is con-centered—with the ultimate, the cosmic center. Her consciousness is a detached concentration. Death has concentrated her, made a center out of her, and only the center matters. The rest detaches itself.

Her heart cries absence. She is the winter of feminine images in the soul. Stark. Stripped. Soul wrung in a rage of cold winds. The stripping begins to disintegrate her identity. She is pieces of her former self. The pieces fall away like leaves in a winter wind.

When the widow has possession of womansoul, the disintegration of identity is difficult not only for the woman herself but also for her friends and family. Fearing their own loss of the widowed woman, those who surround her often insist in both subtle and overt ways that she build a new life out of the pieces of the lost one. A friend will pick up a facet of identity that has slipped from the soul of the widowed woman, clasp it tightly, hold it out, and insist: "This is who you are! Take this beauty on again and remain the one I knew and loved! Don't be crazy!

Don't let go of your self, too; it was bad enough to lose your husband! Hold on to yourself, woman! If you lose any more you will go mad!"

But nothing more can be lost. Everything is already gone. The wisdom of the widow is the Via Negativa: that acceptance described by Matthew Fox in *Original Blessing* as letting the nothingness be nothingness, the pain be pain, the loss be loss, the emptiness be emptiness. There is a kind of freedom here. I remember that some weeks after my first husband died I was driving my car to the Poor Clare Monastery for Sunday Eucharist when I suddenly realized that it didn't matter if I had an automobile accident and died. I didn't fear my death at all anymore. I also was so detached from everything and everyone in this world that I was unhampered by any impending sense of loss in never seeing them again. It is this detachment from all that surrounds and this dis-integration within that gives the widowed woman such an aura of strangeness and mystery. She has been estranged, made a stranger, from the ordinariness of life.

Absence motivates her, the memory of the husband, the recollection of having once been carried through. But now the carrying through, if it comes again, seems cosmic. The widow, concentered in the underworld, feels coextensive with the entire world-without-end. She has a premonition of being cosmic. Her bodysoul, having become universally sensate, shares an instinct with the wholeness of being. She is at the still point of the cosmic dance, "but do not call it fixity," we are reminded by T. S. Eliot, "where past and future are gathered." She is the eternal woman, where past and future are gathered into the present moment. She *is* the present moment.

The woman possessed by the image of the widow lives a precarious existence, especially at the beginning of the possession. This is true for all forms of widowhood: the radical widowing brought about by a husband's death; the lengthy and exhaustive widowing brought about by a husband's chronic illness or emasculation; the widowing thrust upon a woman by a husband's betrayal, abandonment, or divorce. The time is precarious because the woman's own survival is at stake. A drive toward literalizing the descent to the underworld that is characteristic of widowhood is strong. The woman wants literally to die. The decision to survive is a decision made against all her instincts.

To find the courage to make that survival decision, the woman must stand on the edge of the sheer precipice of death and gaze into the opaque dark of her lostness. She must *see* her widowhood. Then she must approach the widow image—black- and blood-clad in the draped garments of mourning—and embrace her. In that embrace the loss becomes sacred, and the widow image transforms to reveal the face of Wisdom.

This transformation brings the Wisdom of resurrection—the reconciliation of the opposites of death and life. In the widow individual death transforms into cosmic life. She experiences a new marriage that involves the entire universe. The masculine and feminine energies within her she recognizes as universally alive—as the energies of the cosmos of which she is both a fragment and a center. She becomes in this consciousness the widow-bride.

The image of the woman in the underworld, the power of the widow to be transformative, is illustrated by the goddesses of the underworld. Ereshkigal-Inanna provides a complex image by combining two goddesses. In this combination we can see the feminine thrust into the underworld, enslaved in the underworld, descending to the underworld by her own accord. She is stripped, she is made powerless, she is both the eye of death and the one who dies. She is impaled on the phallic masculine, she disintegrates, she becomes nothing. In Ereshkigal she groans, weeps, mourns. She brings forth from herself the passion to restore life. She rises and brings springtime and fertility to the world.

Persephone-Kore is widowed by rape before she has been married at all. She is the virgin-widow. She is married to death. But her centered existence in the underworld (the place of the soul) gives her a beauty unattainable anywhere else. When Psyche, the soul, descends to her, she brings back this beauty, which transforms her and makes her immortal.

In Christian imagery Mary is the Pietà and as such is called Health of the Sick, Refuge of Sinners, and Comforter of the Afflicted. For Mary the one who dies is not only her son. The image of Mary–Word of God–Christ Jesus is multivalenced. He is Word to her Virgin self, Son to her Mother self, Bridegroom to her Bride self, and Husband to her Widow self. The Pietà is less an image of a mother losing her son than it is of the whole feminine experiencing the loss of the divine masculine. In Michelangelo's representation of this mystery Mary is large with the power of grief and loss; she is also large with the necessity to be the container within herself of the lost masculine. He will rise. She too must become cosmic. Together they must embrace the world.

Wisdom here is that death is a passageway to cosmic life but it must be traversed. Mary must look upon him who was the totality of the masculine power of the universe in her life and watch him die. In that death she must gaze into the abyss of her loss, of her widowing. She descends into the underworld of her own soul. There is where he rises first. It is in the soul of Mary that Jesus first becomes the Christ. It is in the vast emptiness of the cosmic feminine that the eternal masculine becomes the Cosmic Christ. Together they image the WomanChrist. So we pray to her who is in him and who contains him forever, we pray in faith, in the womanfaith by which the opposites are reconciled both within ourselves and in the world:

> Holy Pietà—*pray for us*
> Mirror of Justice—*pray for us*
> Tower of Ivory—*pray for us*
> House of Gold—*pray for us*
> Ark of the Convenant—*pray for us*
> Morning Star—*pray for us*
> Gate of Heaven—*pray for us*
> Seat of Wisdom—*pray for us.*

Charge to Women

Woman, women all over this land are awakening from unconsciousness and recognizing the vast richness buried in our womanhood; but at the same time we are feeling more deeply than
ever before the multidimensional violence that would keep that
richness buried and uncreative.

You have seen the richness within;
You have dug it from your soul with your bare hands;
You have believed in the Promise of a gentle God
And have been graced.

Now I charge you to awaken women's souls,
To tend our belief in the richness of our womanhood,
To root out the violence that chokes us,
And, by your own becoming,
To be, for all of us, a Promise of Woman-Grace.

Woman, the women cry out.
The women have been shamed.
They have been raped, ridiculed, ignored, abandoned, confused.
The women have endured lies, trivialization, waste of talents and
   gifts.
The women are angry.

You have been blessed to know what anger is.
You are stranger to none of this abuse.
You have screamed out anger at humankind and God,
And you have not been destroyed.
God has received the shaking of your fist as prayer.

Woman, I charge you, by the life you have lived,
To teach us the prayer of anger,
To let us feel in you the power of the anger of God

Against the injustice and the pain we hold:
I charge you to open in us
The door to blessed and golden power.

The women are alone.
They weep themselves to sleep.
They have lost the God of their youth;
They have lost the Companion of their souls.
They have had to reject any God given in oppression in order to
    survive;
But they survive in a vast emptiness.

You have endured the darkness of God.
You have walked through the wilderness of the soul.
You have let yourself become a faceless one before the Unseen
    Mystery.
You have waited for revelation.
And you *have seen*.

Woman, I charge you to be guide through the dark places,
To weep with those who weep,
To hold women who are alone in the vast home of your heart.
I charge you to venture again and again
Into the wilderness
With women who have lost their faces and their God.
I charge you to remember the way.
I charge you to keep the story alive:
    Of the saving presence of God,
    Of the journey's end;
I charge you to light fires and tell the story throughout the night.

Woman, women wonder if the Church can be a community for
    them.
Many women feel excluded, overlooked, judged, found guilty.
Violence has made them stranger in this gathering.

You have heard the Good News the Church can proclaim.
You have listened through all the static of our unwhole systems.
You have claimed the Church for women and you have not let go.

I charge you, then, to be a sign unto the Churches
Of liberation for the oppressed,
Of the grace of womanhood.
And I charge you to be the Church for the women who come into
    your life,
To bear witness to Good News by opening yourself to us
Without judgment.

I charge you to allow yourself to be a witness of transformation:
Of women in the Church, and of the Church by the gift that women
  are.

Woman,
To women laboring to birth a transformed self,
I charge you to be midwife.

To women trapped in abusive relationships,
I charge you to be liberator.

To women whose hope needs your story to survive,
I charge you to tell your story
    Freely,
    Trustingly,
    With courage.
I charge you to be our friend.
I charge you to be priest.
I charge you to be woman of wisdom.
I charge you to hold our belief.
I charge you to tell us the truth.
I charge you to help us find the way.
I charge you to celebrate life.
I charge you to be, with us, a prayer.
I charge you to be, for and with us, WomanChrist.

Notes

CHAPTER 1

1. Colleen McCullough, *The Thorn Birds* (New York: Harper & Row, 1977), frontpiece.
2. Robert Graves, *The White Goddess* (New York: Farrar, Straus & Giroux, 1948), 30–31.
3. T. S. Eliot, "The Dry Salvages" in *Four Quartets* (New York: A Harvest Book, Harcourt, Brace & World, 1971), 44.

CHAPTER 3

1. Diane Wolkstein and Samuel Noah Kramer, *Inanna: Queen Of Heaven and Earth.* (New York: Harper & Row, 1983), 52–64.
2. Wolkstein and Kramer, *Inanna*, 60.
3. Wolkstein and Kramer, *Inanna*, 64.
4. Sylvia Brinton Perera, *Descent to the Goddess: a Way of Initiation for Women* (Toronto: Inner City Books, 1981), 45.

CHAPTER 4

1. Gerard Manley Hopkins, *A Hopkins Reader*, ed. John Pick (Garden City, NY: Doubleday, 1966), 51–52.
2. Graves, *The White Goddess*, 30–31.

CHAPTER 5

1. Dom Gaspar LeFebvre, O.S.B., *St. Andrew Daily Missal* (St. Paul, MN: Lohmann, 1958), 803–805.
2. Wolkstein and Kramer, *Inanna*.
3. Matthew Fox, *Breakthrough: Meister Eckhart's Creation Spirituality in New Translation* (Garden City, NY: Image Books, a Division of Doubleday, 1980), 77.

CHAPTER 6

1. Roger Lipsey, "We Are All Witnesses: An Interview with Elie Wiesel," *Parabola* (May 1985): 27.

CHAPTER 7

1. June Singer, *Androgyny: Toward a New Theory of Sexuality* (Garden City, NY: Doubleday, 1977), 45–46.
2. *Dark Soliloquy: The Selected Poems of Gertrud Kolmar*, trans. Henry A. Smith (New York: A Continuum Book, The Seabury Press, 1975), 213.

CHAPTER 8

1. Adrienne Rich, "Prepatriarchal Female/Goddess Images." in *The Politics of Women's Spirituality*, ed. Charlene Spretnak (Garden City, NY: Anchor Books, Anchor Press/Doubleday, 1982), 36.
2. Richard Wilhelm and Cary F. Baynes, *The I Ching* (Princeton, NJ: Princeton University Press, 1980), 194.
3. Paul Claudel, *Tidings Brought to Mary*, trans. Louise Morgan Sill in *A Treasury of the Theatre*, vol. III, ed. John Gassner (New York: Simon & Schuster, 1935; rev. ed. 1963), 1138–1176.

CHAPTER 9

1. Claudel, *Tidings Brought to Mary*, 1161.
2. Apuleis, *The Transformations of Lucius: The Golden Ass*, trans. Robert Graves (New York: Farrar, Straus & Giroux, 1951), 135.

CHAPTER 10

1. Walt Whitman, "Song of Myself," in *Leaves of Grass* (New York: The Modern Library, Random House, [following the arrangement of the edition of 1891–1892]), 73.

CHAPTER 11

1. Sue Woodruff, *Meditations With Mechtild of Magdeburg* (Santa Fe, NM: Bear & Co., 1982), 42.

CHAPTER 12

1. Margaret Atwood, *Surfacing* (New York: Fawcett Popular Library, 1972), 212–213.

CHAPTER 13

1. Gabriele Uhlein, *Meditations with Hildegard of Bingen* (Santa Fe, NM: Bear & Co., 1982), 92.
2. Annie Dillard, *Pilgrim at Tinker Creek* (New York: Harper's Magazine Press, 1974), 270.
3. Anne Sexton, *The Awful Rowing Toward God* (Boston: Houghton Mifflin, 1975), 62–63.
4. T. S. Eliot, "The Waste Land," in *Selected Poems* (New York: Harcourt, Brace & World), 51.
5. e. e. Cummings, "if I have made, my lady, intricate," in *A Selection of Poems* (New York: Harcourt, Brace & World), 80.

CHAPTER 14

1. Compline, *The Little Office of the Blessed Virgin Mary* (Westminster, MD: Newman Press, 1964), 411.